MUJI
無印良品

First published in the United States of America
by Rizzoli International Publications, Inc.
300 Park Avenue South, New York, NY 10010
www.rizzoliusa.com

MUJI
Copyright Texts © 2010 Ryohin Keikaku,
Authors: Masaaki Kanai, Kazuko Koike, Naoto Fukasawa, Kenya Hara, Takashi Sugimoto
Contributors: Jasper Morrison, John C. Jay, Bruce Mau

For Rizzoli International Publications:
Editors: Ian Luna & Lauren A. Gould
Production: Kaija Markoe and Maria Pia Gramaglia
Editorial Coordination: Marie Iida & Allison Power
Translation Services: Maggie Hohle, Eri Hamaji

Rizzoli International Publications would like to thank Charles Miers and Ellen Nidy

For Hara Design Institute, Nippon Design Center, Inc.:
Project Editor: Kenya Hara
Art Direction: Kenya Hara
Book Design: Kenya Hara, Yukie Inoue, Misa Amako, Shimpei Nakamura
Caption text: Chiyoko Namima
Conversation text: Chihiro Arai

Printed in China

2010 2011 2012 2013 / 10 9 8 7 6 5 4 3 2 1
Library of Congress Control Number: 2010932336
ISBN: 978-0-8478-3487-7

MUJI
無印良品

RIZZOLI NEW YORK

New York, Paris, London, Milan

Image from the "Like Water" Campaign, New York, 2009

Image from the "Like Water" Campaign, Istanbul, 2009

Image from the "Like Water" Campaign, Beijing, 2009

Image from the "Like Water" Campaign, Rome, 2009

MUJI

Not "This is what I want" but "This will do"

Masaaki KANAI | President and Representative Director, MUJI/Ryohin Keikaku Co.,Ltd.

It gives me great pleasure to meditate on the publication of a book about MUJI for a wide, global readership.

MUJI was founded in Japan in 1980 as an antithesis to the habits of consumer society at that time. On one hand, foreign-made luxury brands were gaining popularity within an economic environment of ever-rising prosperity. On the other, poor-quality, low-priced goods were appearing on the market, and had a polarizing effect on consumption patterns. MUJI was conceived as a critique of this prevailing condition, with the purpose of restoring a vision of products that are actually useful for the customer and maintain an ideal of the proper balance between living and the objects that make it possible. The concept was born of the intersection of two distinct stances: no brand (*mujirushi*) and the value of good items (*ryohin*).

MUJI began with three steps: selecting the materials, scrutinizing the processes, and simplifying the packaging. MUJI's concept of emphasizing the intrinsic appeal of an object through rationalization and meticulous elimination of excess is closely connected to the traditionally Japanese aesthetic of "*su*"—meaning plain or unadorned—the idea that simplicity is not merely modest or frugal, but could possibly be more appealing than luxury. By eliminating from products the elements of individual personality and partiality to taste, two things that people were obsessed with at the time, MUJI left room for the individuality of the customers themselves, enabling them to make choices on how they would use the products. Original slogans such as "Lower Priced For a Reason" and "MUJI for Each and Every Person" convey the powerful concept of MUJI that arose from these circumstances, and continue to this day.

Since the very beginning, MUJI has flourished from the support of the many people who identify with its concepts and the products born from those concepts. Clearly, MUJI's development sprang from its pursuit for items that moderate excess and make users feel the beauty and pride in living a simple and modest life. MUJI has not traveled this path alone, however; through continuous communication with our customers, we have walked alongside each and every one of them.

Our products, which we think of as "mature" or "ripened," are the fruits of exchanges with our customers over many years. MUJI's unique products have also evolved through collaboration with designers from around the world. In the beginning, MUJI products arose from conventional products whose materials were reassessed and whose processes were simplified, rather than from a complete redesign. But in the pursuit for ideal products, we have become more aware that

Men's 90-Degree Angle Stripe Socks, 2006.

With their 90-degree heels,
these socks fit perfectly.

Not "This is what I want" but "This will do" | Masaaki KANAI

instead of 'no design,' our products should display extremely sophisticated design that fits naturally into our lives. Designers with outstanding international reputations have granted MUJI the wisdom and insight necessary to produce items like those introduced in this book that are both uniquely simple and useful. In addition, we now cooperate with important manufacturers that boast both history and tradition, such as Thonet. MUJI does not honor the name of the designer of each product we release to the world. This may be why we have been able to naturally establish a mutual understanding of essential ideas with gifted individuals, which I believe result in authentic work.

Looking at the world today, I can clearly see that we are moving toward a time of momentous changes. In the global economy, developed countries have decreased their cruising speed, and in developing nations we see quick progress and expansion. There are plans for new and advanced electricity-centered energy use, and projects promoting the use of renewable resources and more ecologically sensible use of all resources. There is a global awareness and acknowledgement that we need to live reasonably if we are to have a future.

From the beginning, MUJI has held a particular viewpoint on the future of global consumerism, and our vision will not change. Our goals are to suppress extravagant appetites, as expressed in "This is what I want," positing instead a value system for modest living, expressed as "This will do." This desire for moderation is something to be proud of. We hope to share our way of thinking with as many people around the world as we can.

MUJI carries several thousand products in categories supporting the core areas of life: clothing, household goods, and food. Last year we established a research lab called, "The Laboratory of Superior Items for Living," to communicate with customers through MUJI stores and the MUJI website, to develop products, and to promote a way of living that is more comfortable, because it is ultimately more sustainable. Our identity is shaped through a continuous assessment of both newly developed and existing products, as expressed by our motto, "Repeat the Origin, Repeat the Future." A residential project called MUJI HOUSE has also been making progress in recent years, and, in some parts of Japan, groups of these houses are beginning to develop into small neighborhoods.

The contents of this book are a curated document of MUJI's activities. The photographs used are those that have been produced for advertising and PR, and the text, written by members of MUJI's advisory board, uses the same words

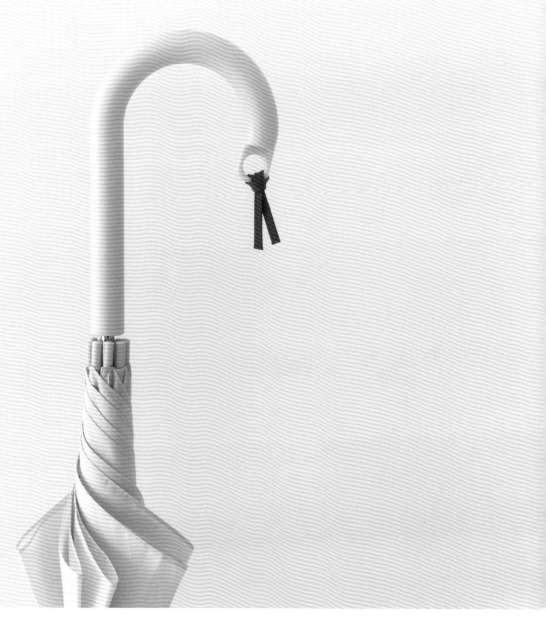

Remarkable Umbrella, 2006.

A personal marker in the hole of
the handle turns an ordinary umbrella
into my umbrella.

we use naturally in discussions about the vision we have for MUJI. The spirit behind these processes is faithfully represented by the words in this book.

For its thirtieth anniversary, MUJI would like to expand further afield,
and not merely in market reach. There are MUJI stores in 18 countries and ter-
ritories in Europe, Asia, and North America. Our hope is that we will one day be
of help to people in many more countries, a resource at their fingertips, much like
the water that we all need.

Not "This is what I want" but "This will do" | Masaaki KANAI

MUJI is good for you

Jasper MORRISON | Product Designer

My father was in the advertising business, and one of his clients was the Irish Brewery, Guinness. When I was about eighteen years old, before I went to design school, he arranged a job for me at the London brewery. My job was to design Guinness products for the African market, where it was believed that the beer had the magical power to improve the manhood of anyone who could afford it. The advertising slogan for the company at that time was "Guinness is good for you," and in fact it had been proved by doctors that Guinness was good for you, so they started to give it to the patients in hospitals. When MUJI asked me to write something about the company I remembered this phrase because there seemed to be some parallels between the beer company's outrageous claim, which turned out to be an honest one, and MUJI. Can a company be good for you? I think so.

In a world where everything is marketed and calculated to be a best seller (even if very few succeed) it is surprising to find a company which takes an opposite approach with the products they offer. Stripping things down, reducing form and colour and denying them the primary role which they usually have would seem like a sure way to lose sales. Such a "philosophy" could never have been developed in the west, where to sell anything you have to shout louder than your neighbour, and where the marketing department controls everything, including the president. So it's no surprise to find that this company's origin is Japan, a country with the strongest tradition of sensibilities in aesthetics and daily life.

There are critics who would argue that the MUJI concept is just another marketing theme, exploiting a niche in the market for those who may be tired of all the other marketing themes. This may be true if you think of the glass of water being half-empty, but to the one who sees it half-full, MUJI is genuine. If you take away MUJI there is a big hole which nothing else can fill. If the MUJI concept is just another marketing theme then how come there are no others copying it as they do every other theme which has originality?

As a public company there's no question of MUJI operating like a charity, and yet for the consumer there's an impression of generosity: not just economic, but also conceptual. A typical MUJI product has just a small bit of extra thought which aims to be helpful to the customer, like the marker pen which is wider at one end than the other, signalling clearly and simply the thickness of the marker stroke at each end, or the towel with a detail which divides the whole into smaller squares which allows it to be cut up into floor cloths when it's useful life as a towel is up. These are just two examples. Other MUJI products may express their concepts less

pp 025-026
left to right:
Cutlery—Table Fork, Dessert Fork,
Table Knives, Dessert Knives, Butter Spreader,
Table Spoon, Dessert Spoon, Tea Spoon,
Soup Spoon, Long Spoon, 2007.

A series of cutlery with thoroughly
considered details: angle, balance,
ergonomics, and form.

visibly, and yet in use, over time, show another kind of generosity, the type which comes from doing a job well for a long time without complaint.

So how can MUJI be good for you? Generally speaking, things are not good for us; too many or too valuable and we are corrupted. But, we all need some things (even Gandhi had a pair of spectacles, some sandals, a bowl, a dish and a pocket watch) and to some extent we are defined by our choices of those things. We may reveal to others in our choice of things that we have good taste or bad taste, expensive taste, cheap taste, modest taste, flashy taste, snobbish taste or no taste at all. Between the moment of choosing and paying for something and the day we no longer have a need for it, there are certain exchanges between the thing and us. The service provided by the thing on the one hand and how we feel about being its owner on the other hand. For some, owning a Ferrari may be the most important thing in life, but is owning something which only a few others can afford good for you? I don't think so.

There is an English importer of wine which has been selling Bordeaux wine in England for more than 300 years, and besides all the expensive wines that they offer, there's one which they call "Good Ordinary Bordeaux," which costs much less than the others but which is fine to drink as an everyday wine. Similarly, the MUJI concept is to make things as well and as cleverly as possible at a reasonable price, for the thing to be "enough" in the best sense of the word, and this kind of "enough" is good for you because it removes status from the product/consumer equation and replaces it with satisfaction. The kind of satisfaction that you have when the money you exchange for the thing is proportional to the value which you receive from the thing, and the thing itself is good at being itself without any pretension of being anything more special.

MUJI is good for you | Jasper MORRISON

MUJI: Reinventing the Future

John C. JAY | Creative Director

For 30 years, MUJI has defied the conventions of product design and marketing. The founding visionaries who saw a future for everyday products by reducing, rather than increasing, their allure, helped to redefine consumer expectations through the refined lens of Japanese culture.

What is remarkable about the MUJI success story is the longevity and breadth of its philosophy as a business model. This modesty survives today despite serious growth issues as it transitioned into the 21st century. From 1999 to 2001, MUJI was on a downward spiral, losing money for the first time in its history, shaking the self-confidence of its creators and loyalists.

Growth and change will challenge the future of any long lasting brand and how a brand evolves is not for the faint of heart or those who fear new ideas. The ability to initiate risk is the mark of any great leader but MUJI had to rediscover its *raison d'être* in order to move forward.

No living brand can afford to stand still. Culture, consumers, investors and competition will constantly challenge you and if you do not strategically reinvent yourself, the competitive landscape will force change upon you. It is romantic for designers to think that something they created can be relevant forever, but history usually proves other-wise. In our lifetime, there are singular products that can stand the test of time and be considered quintessential. However, MUJI is more than a single item and function; it is a vast collection of ideas based upon a single theme of no branding. The challenge is not simply to exist but to grow in relevance...to continuously lead and be a brand of the future. No degree of philosophical posturing, art school naïveté, intellectual voodoo or hiding your head in the sand can ever take away the truth; evolution and change is inevitable...even for MUJI.

The great irony is of course that the "no brand" idea has spawned a very successful global brand, which remains the darling of the design elite. But the design elite alone cannot sustain its future. Today, much to the chagrin of the purists, MUJI advertises on the TV in Japan, and sells globally on the internet, while increasing its retail promotions as new doors open in New York. No logo is no longer enough.

The MUJI initiated 30 years ago existed in a vastly different world. It was born on an island. The era was pre-internet, pre-twitter, pre-cynicism, pre-bailout and pre-Uniqlo as we know it today. In 1980, the brand started with 40 products ranging from food to sundry items, from canned salmon to toilet paper. Today, approximately 7000 items bear the no-logo style of MUJI. The challenge is not simply the great number of products in its inventory, but how a growing brand can stay true to its roots.

The recycled paper notebook is
a MUJI staple. The cover is plain,
the pages non-directional.

A do-it-yourself planner.
You can start anytime.

MUJI's growth in the United States is an exciting moment for the brand... not simply for the legions of old fans and new consumers but for what this challenge can bring to the longevity and evolution of MUJI's legacy and future. The MUJI-brand clearly is at a crossroad. The New York expansion is challenging but potentially rewarding; this is a city that explodes with creativity through the conflict and power of cultural and economic diversity. To survive in New York, you cannot be meek: the city demands a personal point of view. Here, the real elite are the young and the restless. The city offers the tension that all creative people live for and nothing is as invigorating or inspiring than the chance to fail. For MUJI, the craziness of New York is the perfect kitchen for experimentation and connection to a new generation.

Perhaps the greatest challenge facing MUJI in America is all about price and the important balance of quality and cost. Growth brings the spotlight on MUJI's pricing at a time when Americans are wrestling with the concept of the "new normal." What is a contemporary consumer's threshold for spending for thoughtful design and what is the relationship between value and values? How are the higher prices for MUJI products in the U.S. affecting the consumer's relationship to the brand?

Global brands today need to be proactive; they have to be engaged with society and consumers through their management and advocates. Social media has increased the stakes of brand integrity. Young consumers demand transparency in order to measure a brand's actions versus words, and the dialogue is a dynamic two-way conversation which is immediately global. This is especially evident in areas of social responsibility for any corporation. To propose MUJI as an environmentally friendly company in the early 80's is quite different from the scrutiny and standards of sustainability today in the open access world we live in.

Relevance of any brand depends on culture and the evolution of society. How far can the MUJI brand stretch? The legacy of MUJI will rest on its ability to live up to its founding values while finding new consumers to grow not just in sales but in quality, principles and ideas. MUJI has the opportunity to fearlessly lead a new generation to a higher ground through, not despite, consumerism and design.

MUJI began this 30 year journey by trusting the intelligence of its consumer. That trust will always serve them well.

Happy birthday, MUJI...the future is yours.

Meeting MUJI inspires optimism

Bruce MAU | Director

In their honest approach we discover an opening—a way to live with modesty and clarity in the spirit of beauty and intelligence. MUJI began as an idea, and has been exploring and developing this way for 30 years.

As a company, MUJI got it right. They understood that their culture was a design project, and the design of their founding idea would design everything else they would do, including their products.

Since the beginning, they have not only believed in their idea, but also acted on their belief in the holistic possibility of design—a generous practice that connects simplicity and beauty with the intelligent efficiency of material, energy and resources. This approach to the culture of design is not only aligned with the smartest business practice and lowest cost, but also with ecology and nature.

It has been this way since the start. They applied their holistic approach, the MUJI idea, to everything they do, from the embedded intelligence and value in the products themselves, to their elegant and generous approach to communication. It all begins with simple dignity in the idea that the citizen—defined not merely as a consumer—is intelligent and empowered, and deserving of our best.

You may enter MUJI because you support their progressive mandate, or their environmental intelligence. However, you will return to MUJI again and again because you discover that everything they provide is delightful. That's the true genius of MUJI. They embed intelligence in desire. They make smart things sexy. MUJI shows us a better way by demonstrating a new form of exuberant restraint. Advanced simplicity. Simple genius.

By creating a world in this new way, MUJI has been rewarded with a rare kind of loyalty. Because they have quietly created this new way of being in the world, they have been embraced. From 40 to over 6500 products, MUJI has expanded their offering—always true to their idea. They continue to create more and more in this new spirit, building a world of possibility. Not by perpetuating or encouraging a cycle of consumption and waste but, rather, by encouraging a kind of consumption that is sensitive to the act of consumption itself. MUJI allows us to become aware of our own behavior, without judgment, in a way that improves our lives, that demonstrates possibility, and that adds elegance and beauty.

MUJI gives us a glimpse into a world where consumption doesn't equate with destruction, nor pleasure with guilt. It's fashionable to talk about how we can make things smarter but still beautiful, sexy but still environmentally responsible, but MUJI has actually done it. The power of MUJI lies in the fact that you need not know about what lies at the heart of their philosophy. Their products connect to our deepest needs, and by simply choosing to participate in their world we make ours a better place. That MUJI not only exists, but continues to thrive and grow ought to inspire optimism in anyone.

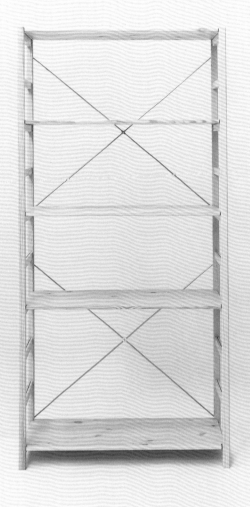

Pine 5-Shelf Wide Unit, 2008.

A shelf unit of pure pine
with distinct knots and grain
and minimal coating.

A testament to the power and importance of the founding idea is this simple fact: even after 30 years, MUJI is still a pioneer. Not an anti-brand, but a non-brand: an open space in the public imagination, a place where I can live my life as I imagine it. I can define my world in a way that is not dominated by the cultural signal of others. I can hear myself think. I can live free. In a world dominated by domination, this idea is so unique, so unorthodox, that we still have no language for it. MUJI exists in a category all on its own.

Perhaps MUJI is a verb: I love to MUJI.

Meeting MUJI inspires optimism | Bruce MAU

1 The Birth of MUJI

Kazuko KOIKE | Creative Director

Lower Priced For a Reason

It's a December day in 1980. A black-and-white single-page ad in Japan's leading paper attracts public attention. It shows a classical line drawing of a hand, like those found in historical dramas seen on the stage or on TV, holding a placard reading, "無印良品".

What is this four-character word? How is it pronounced? Readers searching for answers to these questions are lured into reading the detailed text introducing the various products, and soon learn that the descriptions are actually rational explanations of how each product can have such a low price. The four-character word, *Mujirushi Ryohin*, translates directly as "no-brand superior items:" quality products without a brand. The slogan in the headline is "Lower Priced for a Reason."

This is how MUJI made its public debut in its homeland before it turned into what it is today: a product line known around the world, affecting peoples' lives throughout Europe, Asia, and North America.

There were a total of 40 products, including such items as bulk packages of tissue and toothbrushes, dried and broken-up shiitake mushrooms, slightly crumbled boiled salmon, and bits and pieces of bar laundry soap, all of which were items most contemporary domestic manufacturers overlooked and often excluded as retail merchandise.

One reason MUJI was able to offer this kind of product lineup was that its parent company at the time was Seiyu, a supermarket operator well-versed in prod-

われ椎茸、と書いた袋も登場します。
西友の、むじるし・りょうひん群。
椎茸なら、大小いろいろのサイズがあったり、
割れたものも入っているという一袋。
これが、お安いんです。見場を気づかって
選別する手間に、経費をかけていませんから。
無印良品。わけあって、安くお手渡しできる品々。

食べものならおいしく、日用品はしっかり
役に立つことを原則に、西友が揃えました。
ブランド名や包装にたよらず、
モノを選びとる。それは、たくましい生き方にも
結びつく、大切な視点だと思います。
食品、日用品あわせて31種。とりあえず
ご紹介します。良品が安い、その理由から。

素材の選択──原料の仕入段階で、
まさに工夫をこらします。可能な限りの情報と
経験を生かし、良品の必要条件をみたす。
早く、大量に素材を確保することで
低価格が実現します。
工程の点検──われ椎茸の例のように、
粒ものの大小選別などの手間をはぶく。

本当に必要な工程だけを生かします。
今まで見過ごしてきた部分を活用できる
食品もあります。
包装の簡略──日常どんどん使うものに、
高価な包装は不要です。容器など共通に使える
デザインは生かす。数をまとめられるものは一括。
そして商品名だけを明記してあります。

わけあって、安い。

素材を選択して安くなった「無印良品」

●煮もの用 しょうゆ──1000ml・¥175
用途を煮ものにしぼると、ぜいたくな原料を
使わなくてすみます。実質本位のこいくち登場です。
●低糖度 ゆであずき──430g・¥188
砂糖の使用量を減らしました。甘すぎるのはどうも
健康に……の声におこたえする、新しい甘さです。
●中国産 ハチミツ──1kg・¥748
菜の花、レンゲ、アカシア。いろいろな花の蜜をブレンド。
楽しめて、輸入原価も安くできる中国産を使用しました。
●黒糖 かりんとう──350g・¥175
甘味の使用をおさえた徳用価格です。蜂蜜もミルクも
使わず黒糖のみの甘さ。健康のためにはバランスを考えて。
●中国産 から付ピーナッツ──270g・¥298/400g・¥398
落花生は、からを割って食べるのが風流。
大粒で、たんぱくな味の中国産を。安くお届けします。
●中国産 バターピーナッツ──180g・¥198
あとを引くおいしさ、ひき受けます。たっぷり
召しあがっても大丈夫。中国大陸の豊かな収穫から。
●信州田舎づくり 味噌(中辛)──1kg・¥178
原料の大量仕入れにより、製造コストがおさえられます。
色・味・香りは変わらず、毎日ほしいお徳用品。
●信州白づくり 味噌(中辛)──1kg・¥178
素材の仕込みを工夫して、早くから、大量に準備した
白みそ。お雑煮の白みそ仕立てにもお役に立ちそうです。
●ソフト パン粉──400g・¥125
原料段階でのコスト安と大袋にまとめた包装で、実質
価格をまもっています。使用後は輪ゴムなどでキッチリ
あけ口を結び、湿気から遠ざけて保存の習慣を。

工程を点検して安くなった「無印良品」

●こうしん われ椎茸──100g・¥568
大きさいろいろ、割れもありますが、風味は
変わりません。煮ものや五目寿司など、調理用に。
●セイロン紅茶 ティーバッグ──50袋・¥438
原茶を粉末にするプロセスを省略しました。煎出はおそく
なりますが、リーフティー同様の風味が楽しめます。
●カナダ産 ズワイガニ──内容総量170g・¥498
カニのボディ部分を使用した料理むきのフレーク状。
サラダやコロッケなど、おそうざいに大歓迎されそう。
●煮込み料理用 マッシュルーム──75g・¥138
茸のかさや石づき部分もムダなく使用しました。
風味も量も、タップリ楽しめます。ソース作りにいかが。
●フレーク 鮭水煮──220g・¥168
形は不ぞろいのサケ肉ですが、おいしさは変わりません。
サケ科のからふとますを使用しています。
●ふだん用 ほうじ茶──200g・¥298
原茶の選別を1回にしました。茶葉に大小はありますが
風味は良いのです。棒・くき茶などもまじりますが
むしろ、茶の甘味をひきたてる役を果たしてくれます。
●フリーズドライ インスタント・コーヒー──200g・¥998
粒のこわれを防ぐオイル・コーティングを省略。
粒は不ぞろいですが、風味は変わりません。

●ふだん用 げんまい茶──400g・¥200
玄米茶は、約50パーセントが玄米です。それをすべて
完全な形で入れることが、経済性を考えました。
破砕米、つまり形のくだけた玄米も。香ばしさに
変わりなし。選ぶ工程をはぶけば、そのぶん、
よぶんにお茶を楽しんでいただけます。きゅうすの
中より、茶わんでいただく時の風味を大切に。
●家庭用 いちごジャム──500g・¥285
完熟イチゴのおいしさ、ご存じですね。
デリケートな粒を選りわけるという手間をはぶいたので、
イチゴの風味がそのまま。ジャムに。パンに
ぬりやすい、なめらかタイプの仕上げになっています。

包装を簡略化して安くなった「無印良品」

●5色 歯ブラシ──5本組・¥198
お父さん。ブルー、妹。ピンク、家族がみんなで使うものは
まとめて、ひと包みに。低価格へのたのしい第一歩です。
●しょうゆ ラーメン──500g・5人分・¥198
●みそ ラーメン──500g・5人分・¥198
ひとり住まいには個別の包装も結構。でもご家族で
わっと、にぎやかにテーブルをかこむ。
そんな時には、いくつものラーメンの束が
消えていく。それで、ご家族用ひと包み。
包装代がおさえられるのもうれしい限りです。
●24皿分 カレー(中辛)──480g・¥328
ご家族用、ひと包み。よく使う料理材料は
経済性を大切にしたいと、願いをこめて。
●詰替用 ティッシュ─5パック(400枚・200組)・¥450
まとめてお徳用。5パックに1個。
詰めかえボックス付き。あとは中身を替えるだけ。
●食器・野菜洗い 台所用洗剤──1000ml・¥178
既製の共通ボトルを使用して、容器代をおさえました。
どんどん使うものですから、経済性を考えて。
●マイルドタイプ 台所用洗剤──1000ml・¥358
お肌にやさしい洗剤も。経済性の裏づけで、いっそう
安心。おしょうゆと同じボトルを使いました。
●台所用 包装ラップ──30cm×50m・¥190
まとめて50メートル。簡易吸収で、お徳用。
低公害のブタジエン樹脂を使用して、粘着率はアップ。
●家庭用 味つけのり──12切5枚70袋・¥1,080
ご家族用ひと包み。まとめて。お徳用サイズ。
朝夕の食卓に。お弁当に。毎日欠かせない味だから安く。
●カラメルぐるみ コーンスナック──100g・¥79
毎日のおやつ、大変ですね。平袋に入れたら、甘い
コーンスナックの、お値段も甘くなりました。
●トイレット・ペーパー──114㎜×65m・12ロール・¥475
あ、もう無いのっ。お手洗いの紙は、忍者のように
消えていく。だからご家族用ひと包み。まとめてお買得。
●かつお 削り節パック──5g×10袋・¥258
朝、昼、夜。お台所でおだしの香りの絶えることは
ないほど。簡単なポリパック。お徳用の品で補充を。
★以上の他にも、さまざまな無印良品のアイデアを検討中です
暮らしを大切にする方への贈りものにも、おすすめしたい品々。
再生古紙を使用した、茶色の包装紙が目印です

一部の店舗では、取扱って
いない商品もございますので、
ご了承ください。
西武百貨店各店では、食品のみ
取扱っております。

株式会社西友ストアー 〒170東京都豊島区東池袋サンシャイン60内 郵便局私書箱第1101号

The Birth of MUJI | Kazuko KOIKE

p 029
"Lower Priced for a Reason."
newspaper ad, 1980.

MUJI's first newspaper ad.
The first 40 items are listed by theme
(material selection, production process
elimination, packaging simplification),
along with the reasons
for their affordable prices.

"Love Doesn't Beautify."
newspaper ad, 1981.

Having just added baby goods and clothing,
MUJI now carried 99 items that addressed
every part of life represented
by the keywords "food, clothing,
and shelter." This MUJI poster explains
how items of good quality are affordably
priced by eliminating unnecessary flourishes.

uct development and, more importantly, with the trial-and-error process of product planning from previous attempts to establish a successful private brand. While Seiyu had the foundation for planning high-quality products that might become a hit with consumers, none had enough popular appeal. However, Seiyu was part of the conglomerate Seibu Saison Group and used an internal product science institute for advice on product planning. Inspired by questions from housewives who were invited to the institute, the company boldly changed its entire way of thinking.

One example of the questions from these consumer surveys was: "Why are the bottoms of the stems always left out of canned mushrooms?" This then alerted product developers to the fact that almost ten percent of edible material was being thrown away and that much could be learned from the consumer's point of view.

Seiji Tsutsumi, the president of Seibu Saison Group at the time, attached a great deal of importance to cultural projects and had hired a group of Japan's top design directors for their public relations and advertising. The central figure of this group was legendary art director Ikko Tanaka (1930-2002). When Tsutsumi first consulted with Tanaka about the private brand, Tanaka suggested monochrome packaging. This single comment, rich in its implications, presaged MUJI's entire early identity.

And so MUJI was born from the harmony between the initial development of a business plan for a new product line, and the vision of an art director.

Love Doesn't Beautify:
MUJI's Message and Identity Take Form

In the 1980's, as Japan's economy boomed and the country reveled in the unprecedented prosperity of an era that later became known as the bubble years, MUJI calmly and consistently broadcast its message of simple values.

The creative team assembled under art director Ikko Tanaka included graphic designer Hiroshi Kojitani, copywriter Kazuko Koike (myself), copywriter Shinzo Higurashi—who led in the naming of *Mujirushi Ryohin*—and interior designer Takashi Sugimoto.

Our entire team took ownership of the vision suggested by Tanaka's keyword, "monochrome," which drove the swift and strong formulation of the company's initial identity. Tanaka, who pointed out that Japanese package design was

becoming excessive, seemed to have decided from the start that if he were to develop a product line, monochrome packaging would be best, as it made a very strong statement against an overly ostentatious era. Though it couldn't be compared to today's environmental movement, at the time, following the oil crises of the 1970s, people were beginning to voice concerns about sustainability. Tanaka acted quickly, and made the decision to standardize the company's logo and message in a specific single color against the background color of kraft recycled paper. This product line, made up of items that had been forgotten or ignored, was to be developed from a different standpoint and with a different intention than that used to create other commercial goods. Packaging that is the color of recycled paper promotes the impression of a simple, sincere lifestyle. Tanaka's design, with the single dark reddish brown logo on that background color, garnered powerful results. MUJI's brand identity was formally established.

As for copywriting, all text on advertising and labels was to focus on simply explaining the product.

The three pillars of MUJI product development were: 1) selecting materials, 2) omitting wasteful production processes, and 3) simplifying packaging. Repeatedly, we pointed out in all MUJI advertising that these three reasons were what made our products affordable.

MUJI garnered support and understanding by focusing its advertising on specific products and their characteristics, expressing an ideology in tune with MUJI's very nature.

For example, under the theme of baby goods, MUJI introduced a bib made of cotton that was carefully selected for its gentle texture against babies' skin. The ad carries a simple line drawing of a naked baby done in India ink by illustrator Yuzo Yamashita. The catchphrase was, "Love doesn't beautify."

"Love doesn't beautify" became MUJI's corporate identity, as it were, and continued to be used in storefront campaigns and various other applications. Empathy with MUJI began to grow and spread among people who were attracted to its simple and modest values.

Another successful MUJI campaign featured an illustration of a salmon that was missing its central section. The fish is saying, "The whole salmon is salmon." The text explains that MUJI's canned salmon includes pieces that taste great despite their appearance, which accounts for the low price.

The origin of the graphic was a rough sketch drawn by a member of the

しゃけは全身しゃけなんだ。

アタマやシッポの近くだって
しゃけはしゃけ。
そこで不ぞろいでもおいしい身を
いかしたフレーク缶が
安くできました。
しゃけの仲間には、われ椎茸や
煮もの用しょうゆ、カレー24皿分
ひと包みなどなど。
わけがあって減価を実現した
「無印良品」群です。
4月発売の新顔も店頭に。

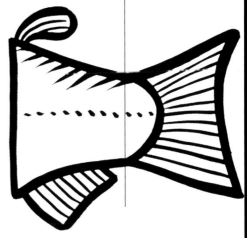

素材を選択して安くなった「無印良品」

●煮もの用 しょうゆ——1000ml・¥175
用途を煮ものにしぼると、ぜいたくな原材料を
使わずにすみます。実質本位のこいくちの登場です。

●低糖度 ゆであずき——430g・¥188
砂糖の使用量を減らしましたので、あっさりした甘さに
なっています。健康と甘さの、グッド・バランス。

●フレーク 鮭水煮——220g・¥168
頭や尾に近い部分を活用しています。身は不ぞろいですが、
おいしさは変りません。おいしく、安くは、ウデ次第。

●黒糖 かりんとう——350g・¥175
甘味の使用をおさえた徳用価格です。蜂蜜やミルクも
使わず、黒糖のみの甘さで、素朴な味が、大好評。

●ソフト パン粉——400g・¥125
小麦粉の配合を工夫しています。色は黒めですが、
味は変りません。揚げもの上手の奥さまに。

●調合 サラダ油——1500ml・¥398
原材料の仕入れを工夫して、なたね油とだいず油が7:3の
割合で調合。おいしい天ぷらのコツは、タップリの油。

●純粋ハチミツ——1kg・¥748
アカシヤやクローバーなどの花蜜をミックスしています。

●徳用 たくあん——400g・¥140
整形のために切り落とした部分を活用しています。
形は不ぞろいですが、おいしさは変りません。甘口です。

★杵つき のり巻あられ——23枚・¥158
最高級のタイ米のおいしさに、日本のノリ・しょうゆを
生かしました。トレーをはずして、包装も簡単にしています。

工程を点検して安くなった「無印良品」

●こうしん われ椎茸——100g・¥568
大きさいろいろ、割れもありますが、風味は変りません。
煮ものや五目寿司など、調理用に最適。
形にこだわらず、おいしさだけを追求した実質価格です。

●煮込み料理用 マッシュルーム——75g・¥138
茸のかさやくきの部分も、ムダなく使用しました。
風味は変わらず、量はタップリ楽しめます。
お子さまの好物オムレツやソース素材にもいかが？

●フリーズドライ インスタント・コーヒー——200g・¥998
粒のこわれを防ぐオイル・コーティングの工程を省きました。
粒は不ぞろいですが、風味は上々です。
カフェ・オ・レやアイス・コーヒーも手軽に楽しめます。

●家庭用 いちごジャム——500g・¥285
粒の大小を選りわける手間を省いています。
完熟イチゴのおいしさを活かして、ジャムに仕上げました。
パンにぬりやすい、なめらかなタイプです。

●2つ割 黄桃——822g・¥198
粒の大きさを揃える手間を省きました。
デザートやケーキの材料に、タップリ使って味覚充実。

●かつお あら節パック——5g×10袋・¥258
いぶして形をととのえる前の荒節を使っています。
包装もまとめて包んで、簡単にしています。
毎日のものですから、味もおねだんも大切に考えたいですね。

●紙ゴミ袋——角底8枚入り・¥140
ラミネート工程を省いていますが、耐水・撥水性原紙を
使用して、耐水には工夫をしました。

包装を簡略化して安くなった「無印良品」

●無し洗剤・衣料用——袋入り2kg・¥548
袋入り、実質価格。パッケージを簡単にして、お安さ実現。

●カレー(中辛)24皿分——480g・¥328
ご家族用ひと皿。包装をまとめて簡単にしました。
大きなお鍋でタップリ作る。煮こんで、翌日も楽しめて。

●詰替用 ティッシュ——5パック・¥450
5パックに1個、詰替用の箱がついています。
装飾ぬきのハイテック感覚が大好評です。

●家庭用 味つけのり——12切5枚70袋・¥1,080
キズのりを使用していますが、味はたしかです。
包装をまとめて、お安くなりました。毎日欠かせない味。

●果汁10% ドリンク——300g・¥58
缶からアルミパックに容器を変えて、お徳用。
オレンジ、パイン、グレープの3種類。凍らせてシャーベットにも。

●トイレット・ペーパー——2枚重ね・12ロール・¥475
まとめてお安く。買いおきタップリで、安心です。

★2倍濃縮 めんつゆ——500ml・¥295
大びん入りで、お安く。天つゆやおだし、茶わん蒸しにも。

★ミルク入り アイス・バー——50ml・8本入り・¥218
まとめてお安い、ひと包み。甘さをひかえた、バニラ味。

★煮出し用 麦茶ティーバッグ——12g×50袋・¥248
煮出しの手間はかかりますが、その分お安く。風味上々。

★バスソープ 棒・石けん——500g・¥208
●洗たく用 棒・石けん——1kg・¥398
包装を簡単にして、ひとつずつ包む手間を省いています。
必要な大きさに切って使えますので、経済的です。

ラベルに安いわけを表示したパッケージ

しゃれてるのね、とおほめの言葉もいただきました。
「無印良品」のパッケージは再生古紙の茶色に一色刷り。
ここでも経費を抑えているのですが、かえってシンプルで
いいとご好評です。飾らない良さを受けとめて
いただいたのが、うれしい。このパッケージが「無印良品」に
こめた西友の提案を、まずお伝えしているからです。
ブランド名や見かけにたよらず、モノの実質を選びとる。
それは買物の仕方というより、たくましい生き方にも
結びつく視点だと思います。
おかげさまで発売いらい4ヵ月、強いご支持をいただいて
充実した「無印良品」。一品一品が確かにお役に立つことを
願って、内容の点検に力を注いでいます。4月には
またバラエティ豊かなグループが仲間入りしています。

●印をつけた商品は、4月新発売「無印良品」の一部です。
●西武百貨店各店は、食品のみ取り扱っています。
●一部の店舗では、取り扱っていない商品も
ございますので、ご了承ください。

SEIYU

西友ダイヤル
03-989-0373
ご意見、ご提案など
お気づきの点がございましたら
ダイヤルをお問いください。
受付時間：午前10時～午後5時

株式会社 西友ストアー
〒170 豊島区サンシャイン60内
郵便局 私書箱第1101号

わけあって、安い。そこで
良品が、無印で登場します。
ブランド名や包装にたよら
ず、モノを選びとる。食品
ならおいしく、日用品なら
役に立つこと、第一。さらに
充実した内容で、西友から。

むじるし・りょうひん。なぜ?
素材の選択＝コストが低く
て良質の原料を確保します。
仕込みの段階で工夫すれば
低価格の良品がつくれます。
工程の点検＝粒の大小を選
んだり、ちょっとした欠けを

よけたりの、工程をはぶく。
食品の、今まで見過ごして
いた部分や新しいおいしさ
の発見にもつながります。
包装の簡略＝ご家族用ひと
包みの大袋や共通デザイン
使用で経費をおさえます。

pp 035-037
MUJI store, Aoyama, Tokyo, 1983.

The first independent MUJI store.
The opening brought intense media
attention. Though a mere 103 square meters,
the shop still thrives today.

project's product development staff, a fine example of the early integration of product planning and graphic campaigns.

At that time in Japan, the trend was toward mass-production by lowering costs, and promoting mass-consumption. According to Setsuo Nakata, one of MUJI's product planners at the time, it was a truly suspenseful adventure to be part of this just-established private brand that was conducting itself in such an idiosyncratic manner, starting with preliminary meetings between product planners and graphic designers, working hand-in-hand with each other through completion.

But contemporary consumers overwhelmingly supported MUJI's "adventure."

This support was due to a combination of circumstances: foreign brand marketing had not yet flourished in the Japanese market; people were disappointed by the significance that was being placed on added value; and Japanese, even in the late 20th century, had maintained their traditional love of simplicity. Proof of consumer support was obvious in the high volume sales of the first independent MUJI store, which opened in the Tokyo neighborhood of Aoyama.

A Whole Lifestyle:
From Single Products to Aesthetics for Life

Japanese use the phrase, "Food, clothing, and shelter," to express an elemental and comprehensive vision of life. The time had come for MUJI to change its strategy of selling MUJI products in Seiyu's various grocery and fashion outlets, often sharing shelf-space with products offered by other companies. The whole MUJI collection needed to appear in a single shop. Aoyama was the location chosen for the first MUJI store for a number of reasons. The primary incentive was that Aoyama was central Tokyo's most competitive laboratory for new and emerging ideas and concepts. Opening there made it obvious that MUJI had become a company that offered an entire lifestyle: food, clothing and shelter. A consistent design policy was apparent in the store layout and paraphernalia.

For the exterior, designer Takashi Sugimoto chose old bricks once used in blast furnaces. The unique texture of the light brown bricks communicated MUJI's philosophy of making things in both space and time. The interior was done mostly in wood, and it was clear that the miscellaneous objects on display, like second-hand buckets, colanders and baskets had been well used by their previous owners.

The Birth of MUJI | Kazuko KOIKE

Sugimoto has said that in designing the first MUJI store, he wanted to keep in mind the stylish aesthetics of fashion boutiques, which were on the rise at the time, while striving to avoid the look of a supermarket, despite the fact that this was a shop selling lifestyle objects for the average person.

It had a different "mood," says Sugimoto. To open the first independent store in Aoyama just three years after MUJI's debut was a truly decisive step. The executive board supposedly had several possible locations in mind, but its members were persuaded by the strong opinions of the design team; some of them had studios in Aoyama and were immersed in the vitality of the neighborhood.

At the time, other brands had established flagship stores in Aoyama, and the people who lived and worked there were creative individuals with sophisticated tastes, making it an active, working community. This was the perfect place for the first store, because the locals would relate to MUJI's ideology and react quickly. The outcome was highly anticipated, as the media support generated through such an influential demographic was momentous.

With the Aoyama store, MUJI tested the waters: 1) questioning received ideas on Japanese and international brands, 2) developing products as a refutation of some of these ideas, and 3) carrying on a discussion about its own existence using labels like "antithesis" or "antiestablishment." This allowed MUJI to create a prototype for developing subsequent stores. The prototype was to present, in a carefully organized single space, a collection of single items with clearly stated features, and through this collection, to demonstrate the aesthetics of a whole lifestyle.

愛は飾らない
無印良品

色のまんま。

羊のまんま、らくだのまんま、人間のまんま。生きものの色は、おおらかであたたかい。無印良品は、まんまの色が大好きです。

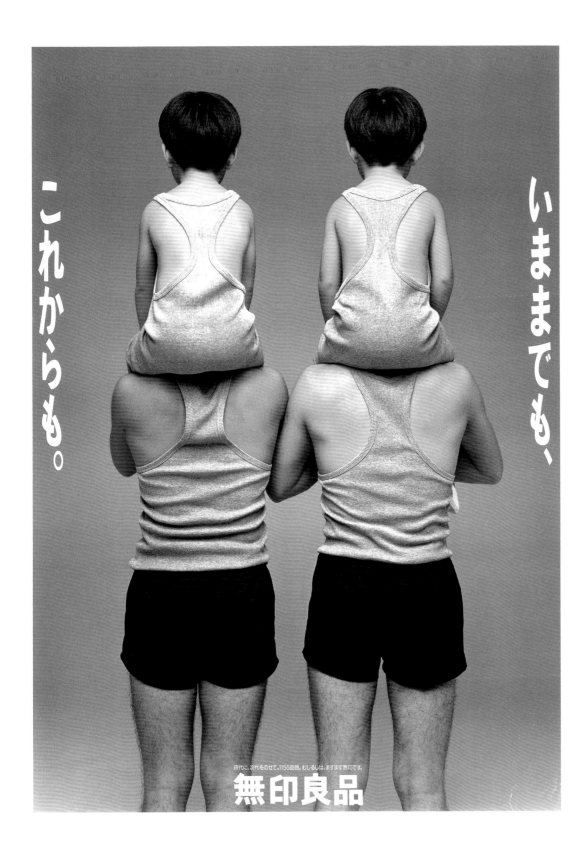

これからも。

いままでも、

時代に、次代をのせて。1155品目。むしるしは、ますます無印です。

無印良品

p 038
"Untouched Color" poster, 1984.

MUJI developed a series of products called
"untouched color," that were made of
unbleached, non-dyed fabrics based on
the colors of animal fur and other
natural materials. This sense of natural
inheritance is part of MUJI's foundation.

"Until Now, and From Now On"
poster, 1984.

As MUJI developed more children's clothing,
this poster expressed MUJI's intention of
spanning the generations, supporting
the lifestyles of a variety of people.

The Birth of MUJI | Kazuko KOIKE

もっと愛される
自転車になりたいと。

無印良品

株式会社 良品計画 ｱｰﾄ○ 東京都豊島区東池袋四丁目二十六番三号

チェーンを使わないシャフトドライブ方式の採用で衣服の巻き込みや裾汚れの心配を
なくした自転車を、無印良品は、さらに一歩進めて折り畳み式に。とかく置き場所が
問題になっていた自転車の悩みがずいぶん解消されたわけです。人と自転車がもっと
仲良く住みやすい街にするために、無印良品は自転車を折り畳み式にしました。

どこにでもあるけど
どこにもないもの

"A More Loveable Bicycle" poster, 1993.

This compact bicycle, equipped
with a folding mechanism,
solved people's parking problems.
An example of product development
based on urban life, the bicycle takes into
consideration the item's relationship to
both the house and the neighborhood.

今を重ねる。
生活。

ガラスウエアの収納と
バラエティを提案します。

無印良品

株式会社　良品計画　〒一七〇東京都豊島区東池袋四丁目二十七番十号

"A Stack of Moments: Life" poster, 1993.

Stackable wine glasses.
Their ease of use embodies other factors,
such as durability and efficient storage.

The Birth of MUJI | Kazuko KOIKE

"MUJI: Also Found in Portugal"
poster, 1994.

This poster explains the knitwear-making
process, from material to stitching
in Portugal, where it utilizes a traditional
technique using extra fine yarn
that yields beautiful results.

この話の続きは無印のお店で

無印良品

株式会社 良品計画 〒一七〇 東京都豊島区東池袋四-二十六-三

インドから
教えられたこと。

たとえば、それは南インドでつくられている手織りの
綿布の素晴らしさです。機械化とか技術革新とは無縁の
手織りの綿布には、人の手を介した温もりと味わいが
今も変わらず生きています。夏を、暑さのなかを涼しく
過ごすための理想的な布地、それをインドの人たちは長
い歴史のなかで見つけ、今も変わらず伝えてきました。
無印良品はインドから、そんなプリミティブな手織りの
綿布の素晴らしさを学びました。夏の衣料品や家庭用品
の一部を、無印良品はインドで生産しています。伝統の素材
と縫製技術を生かしながら、良い商品をコストをおさえア
つくれる インドに学び インドに教えてもらったことを、
無印良品は海外一貫生産というカタチで生かしています。

（夏の知恵
　インド手織り）

"What We Learned from India"
poster, 1995.

This poster explains that MUJI,
having discovered the magnificence of
India's ancient hand-woven cotton,
will manufacture summer clothing
and home goods in India.

The Birth of MUJI | Kazuko KOIKE

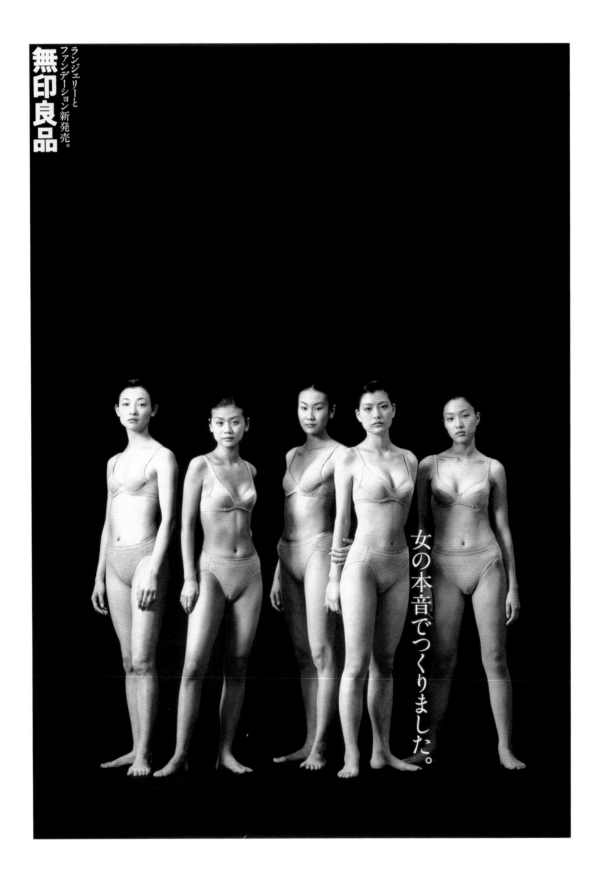

"Made from a Woman's Point of View"
poster, 1996.

With the debut of undergarments
and lingerie, MUJI broadened
its range of goods for women.

無印良品は
インドに
恋をしています。

もう、10年近く前から、無印良品はインドの織り物を日本に紹介してきました。素材としての素晴らしさをインドから頂き、無印の目を通してつくった衣料品や家庭用品たちです。夏の蒸さを凌ぐための知恵がインドの織り物プリミティブな技術で織られた布地。その独特の風合いからは、忘れかけた素材の温もりが今も変わらず伝わってきます。織り物の布地の原点はここにある。だから、無印良品はずっとインドに思いを寄せているのです。（インドの織り物には豊さを凌ぐ知恵がある）

無印良品

"MUJI Loves India" poster, 1996.

Captivated by India's cotton fabrics
and the way they regulate heat
during summer, MUJI continues to
incorporate the material into its products
and introduce them to Japan.

p 046
"Essential Quality" poster, 1997.
p 047
"Essential Features" poster, 1997.

Sweet potato chips and cardboard
storage boxes. Introducing products
that maximize the original flavors
or appearances.

The Birth of MUJI | Kazuko KOIKE

素質。

無印良品

素材の質を、素顔の魅力を、素直に
生かした商品たち。

素顔。

無印良品

素材の質を、素顔の魅力を、素直に
生かした商品たち。

The Birth of MUJI ｜ Kazuko KOIKE

"The MUJI Wind Blows in London and Paris"
poster, 2000.

One of a three-part series of posters
reflecting on MUJI's history for its 20th
anniversary, this explains that, since its
1991 London debut, MUJI has advanced
into important cities around the world
with 14 stores in the UK, and five in France.

MUJI Conveys Culture:
The International Development of 無印良品

In 1989, MUJI became an independent joint-stock corporation called Ryohin Kei-kaku. [Translated literally: Superior Goods Planning]

With the bubble economy at its apex, and with MUJI receiving numerous domestic requests to open more stores, a letter arrived from the manager of the established department store Liberty of London, which stated, in part:

We have been visiting and observing the MUJI store in Aoyama for the past five years, and we highly value the contents of your products from Japan. Our company would like to ask you to consider opening a store in our London branch as a project commemorating our anniversary. We have always studied and introduced Asian culture, and currently we consider MUJI as our one and only stimulation from the East.

So MUJI made its overseas debut in London in 1991. During the preparation stage, the UK staff said it would very much like to use the Japanese phrase *Mujirushi Ryohin*, written in the Roman alphabet, with the nickname being "MUJI." In Japanese, 無地 (pronounced "*muji*," but not using the same characters used in "*mujirushi*") means something in a single, solid color, with no pattern, or refers to that characteristic. This concept underlies the spirit of MUJI, so the creative team in Tokyo agreed. For its world market debut, 無印良品 became "MUJI."

Why was MUJI welcomed in Europe, North America, Asia, and other parts of the world, where it opened subsequent shops? To put it simply, it's because MUJI conveys a look and feel that is Japanese in origin.

The nature of the MUJI concept—its simplicity, an unadorned integrity, and the way a MUJI product blends into a living space without asserting itself—all of these qualities are common in traditional Japanese architectural space. For example, compared to a simply "plain" Western interior space, a *tatami* room with *shoji* latticework and paper doors, void of furniture, exhibits a more "reductive" beauty.

Because MUJI's product planners propose objects that are as plain as possible while still adding to the comfort of the customer's lifestyle, they convey more cultural values than just "simplicity."

The polypropylene product line has the "plain" pedigree, but it also presents the aesthetics of a contemporary Japanese lifestyle embodied by concepts like "Cool Japan." Critic Donald Richie points out that back in the Edo period (1603-1868), to be "cool" was to show some "*iki*," variously translated as, "style, refinement, or sophistication." MUJI fans in France certainly sense MUJI's "*iki*" as "chic."

In his introduction to the aesthetics of "*iki*," Richie defines frankness and unpretentious charm. (Richie, Donald. *The Image Factory: Fads and Fashions in Japan.* London: Reaktion Books, 2003.) The important industrial designer and thinker Sori Yanagi codified key doctrines of the Japanese lifestyle to the world, including the notion of *yo-no-bi* (the balance between form and function) and the promotion of anonymous beauty. As a successor of sorts to Yanagi's legacy, MUJI exports a unique conception of quality from Japan to the world.

ロンドンに、パリに、MUJIの風が吹く。

日本発の良品群がロンドンに登場して8年
いまはパリの街角にもなじんでいます。
無印のなまえから生まれた愛称「MUJI」
無地、プレーンに通じる意味が利いて。
さすがライフスタイルと価格に厳しい二都の
市民の選択です。ぜひお立ち寄りを。

無印良品

株式会社 良品計画 〒170-8424 東京都豊島区東池袋4丁目26-3 http://www.muji.co.jp

イギリス MUJI
オックスフォード ストリート・ロンドン、オックスフォードサーカス駅 徒歩3分
カーナビー ストリート・ロンドン、オックスフォードサーカス駅 徒歩5分
ティー・シー・アール・ロンドン、トッテナムコートロード駅 徒歩3分
ロング エーカー・ロンドン、コヴェントガーデン駅 徒歩3分
シェルトン ストリート・ロンドン、コヴェントガーデン駅 徒歩3分 ニールストリート界隈
ケンジントン・ロンドン、ハイストリートケンジントン駅 徒歩3分
キングス ロード・ロンドン、スローンスクエア駅 徒歩3分 マークス&スペンサー横
ホワイトリーズ・ロンドン、ベイズウォーター駅 徒歩5分 ホワイトリーズショッピングセンター内
トラフォードセンター・マンチェスター、マンチェスターピカデリー駅 トラフォードセンター内
キングストン・サリー、キングストン アポン テムズ駅 徒歩7分 ベントールセンター内
ブルーウォーター・ケント、グレートハイアム バリ 6分 ブルーウォーター内
レディング・レディング、レディング駅 徒歩5分 オラクルショッピングセンター内
リーズ・リーズ、リーズ駅 徒歩5分
フランス MUJI
サンシュルピス A・パリ、サンシュルピス駅 徒歩5分 サンジェルマン・デ・プレ界隈
サンシュルピス B・パリ、サンシュルピス駅 徒歩5分 サンジェルマン・デ・プレ界隈
オペール・パリ、オペール駅 徒歩1分 オペール通り オ・プランタン横
フォーラム デ アル・パリ、レ・アル駅 徒歩2分
フラン ブルジョワ・パリ、サンポール駅 徒歩5分 マレ界隈

The Birth of MUJI | Kazuko KOIKE

MUJI Glasgow, 1992.

The MUJI store in Glasgow,
Scotland's largest city.

The Birth of MUJI | Kazuko KOIKE

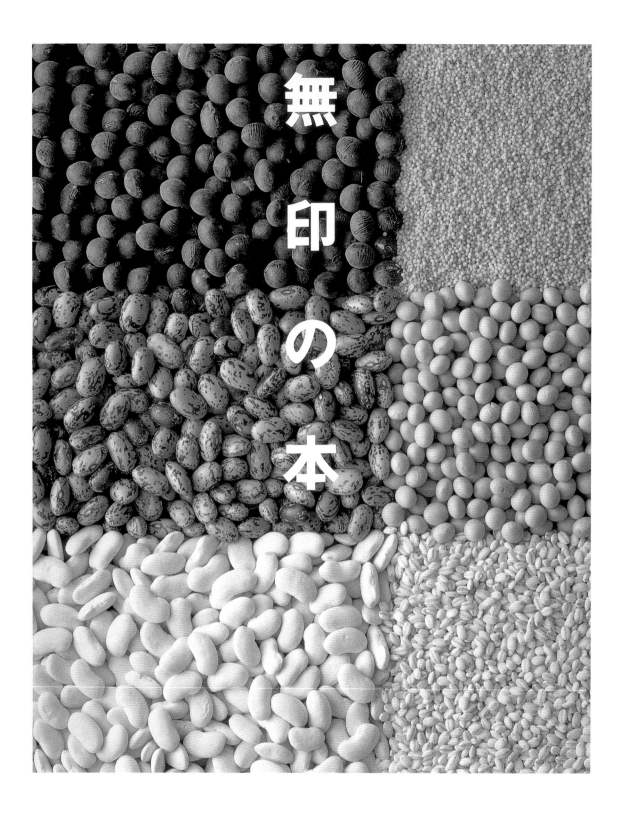

無印の本

"MUJIRUSHI no Hon"
Published by Libroport, Tokyo, 1988.

Summarizing MUJI's underlying approach,
this book is composed of four chapters:
Naturally, Anonymously, Simply,
and Earth-sized.

冬の落葉とウズラの卵。ひとつとして同じ色和、模様もない

29

干してひき出す うまみの知恵

47

火消半纏の粋

73

Top: Fallen leaves in winter, and quail's eggs.
No two are alike in color or pattern.

Center: Dried goods essential to Japanese
cooking. Our ancestors' wisdom:
drying food brings out the flavor.

Bottom: The sophistication of a firefighter's
hanten [traditional short coat] juxtaposed
with dynamic fonts and graphics.

The Birth of MUJI | Kazuko KOIKE

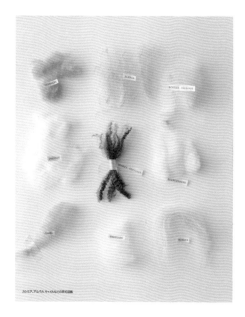

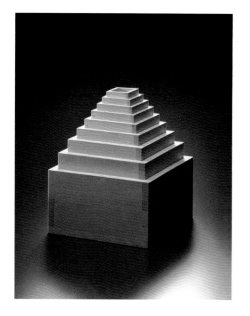

Top: Illustrated index of raw wool, including cashmere, alpaca and camel.

Center: A David Nash sculpture.

Bottom left: A set of masu: traditional measuring boxes used to calculate volume.
Bottom right: Bamboo chopsticks used during celebrations.

紙子の一枚　　小池一子

Top left. Small knives that are
both functional and beautiful.
Top right: Simple brushes for scrubbing
and dusting.

Center: "Kamiko," Issey Miyake's Japanese
paper clothing

Bottom: The Naga tribes of
Northeastern India live as one with nature.

The Birth of MUJI | Kazuko KOIKE

2 Products of MUJI

Products of MUJI

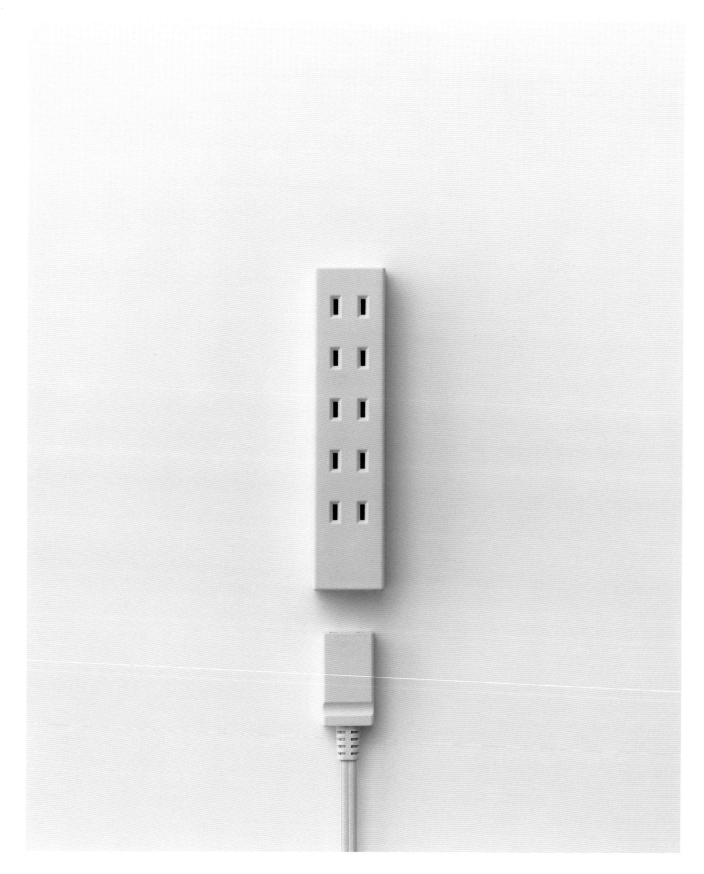

pp 056-057
MUJI House (Renovation), 2004.

Storage proposals for MUJI's
single-module products.

Power Strip, 2006.
Extension Cord Short-Type, 2008.

A series of smart-looking straight-line
electrical outlet strips.
Users can choose the number of
outlets (2,3 or 5) and the length of
power cord (1m, 3m, 5m),
to fulfill a variety of requirements.

Cherry Finish Hall Coat Tree Stand / S · L, 2006.

Made of sturdy beech wood,
it's shaped much like a real tree.

PP Airtight Container / 6L · 20L · 45L, 2006.

Hospitals and other facilities make use of
these durable and airtight containers.
Handy for storing a variety of things,
they are completely impenetrable
by water, odor or light.

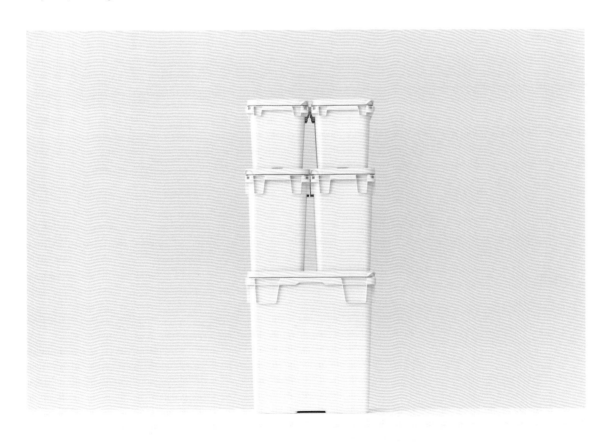

Products of MUJI

Linen Caftan, 2006.

Stress-free casual clothing
like this is worn in arid
regions of central Asia.

Maraca, Mini-Xylophone, Guiro, Bell, Castanet, 2007.

Wooden instruments that make authentic musical sounds, with shapes and sizes that are easy for children to handle.

Organic Cotton Pile Bear-Bracelet Organic Cotton Pile Bear-Mascot, 2007.

Organic cotton toys sensitive to the delicate skin of babies, made free of chemicals.

Long-Sleeved Pajamas with a Belly Band, 2007.

The waistband has been joined with a *haramaki*, the traditional "belly-band" designed to prevent chills. This way, even a child who tosses and turns won't get a cold tummy during the night.

House Type Gift Box / M·L, 2008.

Once the gift is removed, children can play with and draw on the packaging.

Products of MUJI

Ash Bed—Double Bed
Headboard for Ash Bed, 2008.

Depending on one's taste and lifestyle,
the headboard and legs can be
attached or removed.

Bicycle 26-inch, 2009.

MUJI has been making and improving
its prototypical bicycle continuously
since 1982.
The characteristic H-frame consists of
two central supports for the handlebars
and seat connected by a single crossbar.

Electrical Fan, 2008.

The lack of curvature makes it easy
on the eye, even when left in plain view.

**Stainless Steel Non-Chlorofluocarbon
Refrigerator / 375L, 2007.**

Stainless steel, common around sinks
and other water-prone applications,
is incorporated into this refrigerator.

**Skin Toning Lotion for Sensitive Skin
High-moisturizing Action, 2008.**

Made of spring water from *Kamaishi*,
Iwate Prefecture, and free of parabens,
alcohol, perfume, color and mineral oil,
this permeates skin easily.

Polyethylene Hot Water Bottle / S・L, 2008.

Made of lightweight, translucent material,
these come in a variety of sizes
and can be used variously.

**Recycled Double Cotton Key Neck Shirt,
2008.**

Thanks to the use of shorter fibers
that are usually eliminated
in the spinning process (cotton lint),
this shirt feels soft and fluffy.

**Steel Frame, 2008
PP Single Drawer DVD Unit, 2006.
Steel Frame Length Type, 2008.**

Standard MUJI items, these are combined
with a steel frame and enable storage
space to hang unsupported.

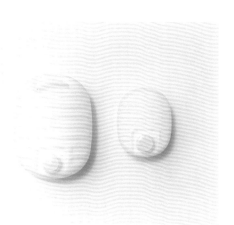

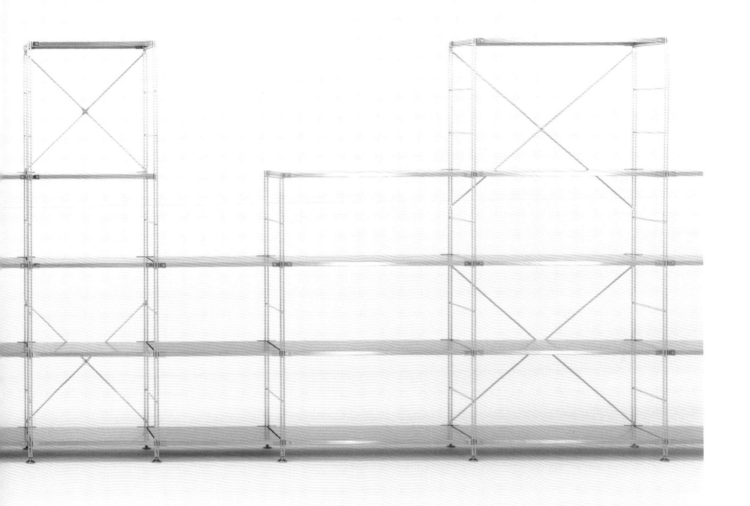

Stainless Steel Unit, 2005.

Developed on the basic dimensions of the *"fusuma"*,
or paper sliding door common in traditional Japanese dwellings,
this is a MUJI basic. Different widths, heights,
and shelf materials can be freely combined.

**PP System Box Lid for Dust Box /
Separating Recycle Garbage /
Lid for Umbrella Stand, 2006.**

A container that can function as a trash bin,
storage container or umbrella stand,
all with the exchange of a simple lid.

**Aluminum Doorknob With Key
Aluminum Lever Handle with Key, 2007.**

A timeless infill product made of aluminum.

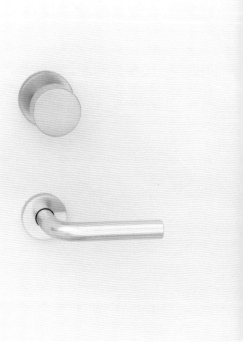

Beige Porcelain Ladle Stand, 2007.
Stainless Steel Ladle, 2005.

Finally, the perfect resting spot for the ladle
during meal preparation; a small dish
with a single indentation adds simplicity to its form.

Steam Fan-Type Aroma Humidifier, 2008.

The chimney allows the direction of
the vapor to be controlled in order to
prevent condensation.

**Rattan Stackable Box S /
Basket S · L, 2007.**

Hand-woven by farmers in northern
Vietnam, these can be stacked.

Canvas Tote Bag, 2009.

The simple form results from
elimination of excess functions
in pursuit of utility.

**Steel Unit with Casters 4 Drawer /
9 Drawer, 2006.**

These thin storage shelves
with 0.8mm-thick steel frames
move freely on four casters.

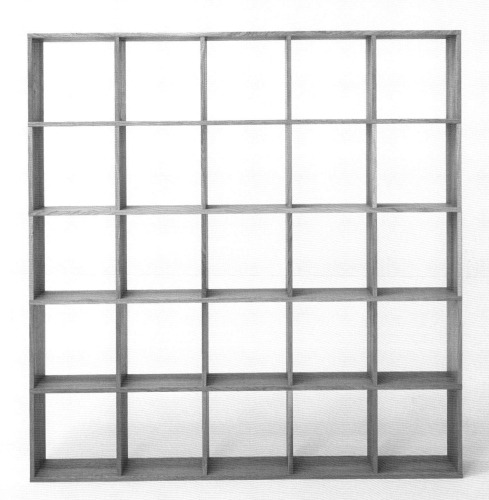

Stacking Oak Shelf, 2009

Combined vertically or horizontally,
this unit can also be used as a partition.

Products of MUJI

**Relaxation Chair with an Ottoman,
Upholstered with an Acrylic Blend,
Plain-Weave Sofa Cover, 2009.**

Cantilevered and making use of wood's natural curvature,
this product was conceived with the image of the legs at the moment
of relaxation. The seat is reclined slightly, allowing the knees to rise.

Products of MUJI

Jute Bag, 2008.

Made from jute, a type of hemp,
it's both ventilated and absorbent,
perfect for storing vegetables and grains.

Unsalted Potato Chips, Wave-Cut Type, 2008.

Unflavored. Condiment powders
(sold separately) allow for
a variety of flavors.

Recycled Kraft Paper Memo Pad, 1996.

A low-priced, easily used standard:
the memo pad. MUJI has been making
products with recycled paper
since its inception.

Organic Unbleached Cotton Pile Towels, 2008.

Made from cotton grown on fields that have been free of
agricultural chemicals and chemical fertilizers
for at least three years prior to harvest.

Mattress-Bed, 1991.

Standard MUJI. A simple form: mattress with legs.

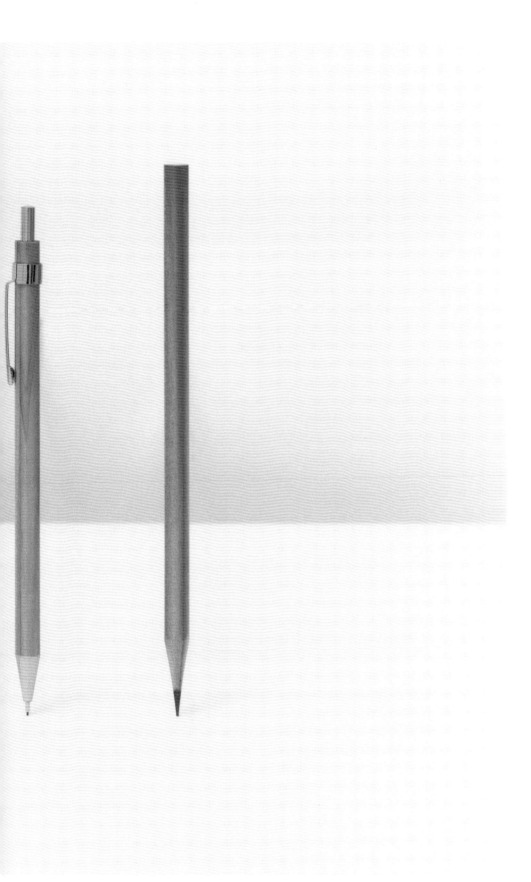

Wooden Hexagonal Mechanical Pencil
Wooden Hexagonal Ball Point, 2009.
Aluminum Ball Point
Aluminum Mechanical Pencil, 2000.
Pencil, 2007.

These hexagonal writing instruments,
like traditional pencils, are easy to hold,
and don't roll off the table.

3 Product Design of MUJI

Naoto FUKASAWA | Product Designer

MUJI is enough

Design can be thought of as a factor that injects a level of excitement into daily life. If we substitute the metaphor "brand" (or *shirushi* 印) for excitement, and then take away the excitement/*shirushi* to create *mujirushi* (無印), or no-brand, we help strike a balance in the world of design. Adopting a critical stance to "ordinary" design, MUJI is devoted to producing functional tools for life. I'm not saying that excitement is bad. We need it and want it in our lives, but there shouldn't be too much. MUJI is a design ideology that occurred naturally as a form of resistance against an era that was seen as chaotic and overflowing with stimulation. Excitement and MUJI represent a pair of opposite desires in our daily lives—or our lifestyles. MUJI carries a sense of comfort that can only be felt when we suppress a desire or longing. It's as if, after searching everywhere for what you want and having no luck, you arrive at MUJI in the end, exhausted. And you think, "I guess this will do." There is a feeling of something slipping right into its proper position that is similar to the feeling of giving something up. It's the feeling you get when you're able to recover a little calm after being in the frenzied state driven by desire, and look around to find a collection of objects that are reasonable or suitable to daily life, waiting quietly for you.

At MUJI, product design is not a medium for emphasizing the individuality or lifestyles of designers or end users. A MUJI product takes an inevitable form, perfected through professional devotion to making tools for living. Its shape is determined by its purpose, and by continuous refinement over a long period of time. MUJI objects don't start out as products, but as familiar tools, truly good products that have withstood the passage of time and continue to be used, and useful. Consider comfort, or the perfect position. What are these, but the essential results of use, testing, revision, and more use? They remain. Because average people participate in the process of refining MUJI products, their critiques are like a stiff breeze that helps MUJI constantly right itself, and clarify the appropriate forms for MUJI products, so that every one maintains MUJI's fundamental ideology.

So it can be said that it is our customers who support our ideas. If something MUJI makes deviates very far from what they consider appropriate to MUJI, their criticism is loud. It has become a distinct asset of MUJI that so many keep strict watch on our ideology. In judging our products, they say, "It's MUJI-like," or, "It's not MUJI-like." The definition can vary, of course, so if the standard is a single

Wall Mounted CD Player, 2001.

As with a fan, tugging the string
turns it on and off.

Product Design of MUJI | Naoto FUKASAWA

vertical line, then MUJI products are constantly and subtly oscillating over the line. It fluctuates between, "gone too far, so come back a little," and, "not quite enough, so add a little more," until, ideally, the oscillation would become so slight that it would culminate in a single line. But I know that the oscillation will never cease.

Background and Splendor (Ground and Figure)

If something flamboyant is the center of attention, the background makes it stand out. The flamboyant object is the figure; what stands behind it is the ground. Each is an integral part of the pair: "ground and figure." There is a general misconception that design is the process of creating the center of attention, but it is actually the important process of creating a world in which background and splendor, ground and figure, can exist as a pair. These are beautiful and in harmony only when they respect one another's positions. Design has flooded our world with figures, things meant to be the center of attention, which is exactly why MUJI is now clarifying its position as the background. In product design, MUJI considers the relationship between ground and figure. If the figure is showy, we must be the ground, or the world will fall into confusion.

If splendor is the human being, then background is his lifestyle. If the living room sofa is splendor, then its surroundings must be designed as the background. If the food is splendor, the plate is background; and if the plate is splendor, the table becomes the background. The harmony that results from each element maintaining its proper position is beautiful. MUJI becomes the background in the lifestyles of its customers. This is why MUJI products blend into a neutral image. MUJI tries to create a background that might at first glance seem commonplace, rather than something that stands out.

Lately, I've even begun to think that if the figure is gaudy, we don't need it at all. There's plenty of beauty and richness in a well-ordered background. If we respect nature, which includes human beings, we see that it's more natural for things to exist subtly. The concept of arranging a lifestyle so that it becomes the background (which is different from *creating* a background) is an underlying current in MUJI's product development. Keeping its designers anonymous; avoiding materials that are bright, shiny, or assertive in color or odor; using natural materials and methods: all of these are expressions of MUJI's intention to devote itself to staying in the background.

Rice Cooker 0.5L, 2005.
Bamboo Rice Paddle, 2002.

The lid has a built-in paddle rest.

Air Cleaner, 2007.

The neutral shape of this appliance is
created by isolating louvers
—familiar as structures for airflow
in many commercial and residential
applications—into a formal gesture.

Shredder, 2007.
PP Dust Box for Shredder, 2004.
PP Dust Box, 2001

This trash bin has a paper shredder
on the underside of the lid.

Ash Bed—Double Bed
Ash Chair, 2004.

The headboard and the chair back are
designed to be at the same angle.
Both are made from Japanese Ash.

**Molded Sofa with Left Arm / Right Arm
Cotton Upholstery Sofa Cover for
Molded Sofa, 2005.**

Unlike in the creation of a conventional sofa,
no material is wasted when using
molded urethane foam.

Left to right:
Bone China Milk Creamer / Tea Pot L /
14cm Plate and Saucer, 2006.
Bone China Coffee Cup, 2005.
Hakuji Porcelain Tea Pot / Soy Sauce Pot /
Rice Bowl L / Round Flat Bowl L /
"Donburi" Bowl L / Bowl / Plate L /
Plate XL, 2004.

Vessels that complement any type of
cuisine and are well suited for everyday use.

pp 095-099
Solid Oak Dining Table, 2007.

The texture of solid wood
only improves with time,
gradually developing character.

We've heard a certain amount of criticism that a lifestyle made up of only MUJI products would be bland, but MUJI earns its respect for striving to coexist with whatever objects are appropriate as the figure, gladly taking on the role of the ground. If MUJI were to begin to make assertive products in an effort to avoid blandness, it would undoubtedly be criticized all the more.

Real Furniture

We call furniture made of pure wood Real Furniture because lots of furniture is made of materials that only *look* like real wood. Everyone maintains that, "what is pure is genuine." Furniture made only of wood is beset with warps, twists, uneven grains, and sharp discoloration, leading to instability in product quality. However, given that this is the natural appearance of the piece, its value increases as it gradually changes over time to blend in with the owner's lifestyle. This value is known as *wabi sabi*, a Japanese aesthetic that emphasizes subdued refinement and the ephemeral. The value of a genuine object is in its ability to get better with each use. Fake things, on the other hand, don't gain character as they age, but simply become depleted.

MUJI came up with the idea of making a series of pure oak furniture called Real Furniture out of the desire to make things that—even as they get scratched and marred—can still be used for a long time: something that actually makes us grow more attached as it ages, so that we can't imagine throwing it away. When we're young, we tend to buy a new set of affordable furniture every time we move, or else continuously add more furniture as our lives change, but people who decide to buy real wood furniture have a growing determination, a resolution within that makes them say, "I am going to live with this furniture from now on." It's natural to want something to grow old with, and MUJI wanted to make furniture that fulfills that wish. Real furniture is actually a very simple combination of wooden boards, more like putting a board on two heavy blocks to make a simple table, designed in the image of a shelf or a floor, both of which act as part of the architecture. This concept is similar to that of traditional Japanese housing, which does not include furniture, and is based on the Japanese ideology that states that any flat plane can have a number of varied uses, allowing the reservation of a certain level of freedom by not restricting its functions. These are not things, but part of a space; they are not assertions, but the background of life. They are "MUJI-like."

Product Design of MUJI | Naoto FUKASAWA

Solid Oak Side Cabinet, 2008.

This cabinet can serve a variety of purposes,
from display case to storage space.

Center: **Solid Oak Bench**
Left and right:
Custom-Made Solid Oak Bench, 2007.

These benches can also be used
as a shelf or rack.
The boards are joined to offset warping,
and every seam is carefully examined.

Wide-Arm 3-Seater Sofa—Double
Feather Cushion
Cotton Upholstery Wide-Arm Sofa
Cover for Double Feather Cushion, 2007.

An abundance of feathers fills
the soft cushions that will envelop you.
Equipped with all the necessary features for
every function, it is perfect for leaning,
sitting or reclining.

Fabric Upholstery Sofa with Oak Legs
Fabric Upholstery Sofa Cover in Hemp
Canvas, 2007.

Plenty of cushioning makes it extremely
comfortable and durable. The cover,
cut from a single piece of cloth, gives it
clean lines and an alluring simplicity.

Tube Chair with a Back Cushion, 2007.

A simple, useful chair made of steel tubing.

Steel Shelf, 2007.

A simply assembled shelving unit,
constructed of steel boxes
and wooden shelves.

Oak Oval Dining Table, 2007.

A thin dining table.
The legs stand at wide angles to
give it additional stability.

Product Design of MUJI | Naoto FUKASAWA

Product Design of MUJI | Naoto FUKASAWA

MUJI Thonet

I believe that MUJI's ideology is universal, and therefore has quite a bit in common with traditional masterpieces. So it makes sense that MUJI would collaborate with Thonet to redesign the standard bentwood chair, Model No. 14, and the bent tubular steel chair designed by Marcel Breuer. Thonet's bentwood chair has a long history as the standard, having been continually and efficiently manufactured in countless numbers. In recent years, however, a dwindling number of successors to the wood-bending technique has raised production costs. MUJI, which will distribute this joint product, is attempting to modify this "chair of the people" so that it can be manufactured at a reasonable cost, as it was in the beginning. As part of its basic production ideology, MUJI intends to make sure that these masterpieces remain popular and affordable. This classic chair, well loved since its 19th-century debut, is the perfect model for future MUJI products. We hope to take traditional master-pieces and help them come to life in contemporary lifestyles instead of producing rare collectors' items, and at the same time take advantage of many more opportunities to collaborate with brands like Thonet.

James Irvine designed the bentwood chair and table and Konstantin Grcic designed the bent tubular steel furniture. Both men have designed numerous master-pieces and deeply support MUJI's ideology. One of Mr. Irvine's design decisions was replacing the inner of the two bentwood pieces on the chair's back with a horizontal crosspiece. When the chair is placed in front of the table, this crosspiece, of the same width as the tabletop, seems to disappear. Such magical design, employing insight to minimize the elements, is typical of MUJI.

Mr. Grcic redesigned a typical bent tubular steel chair and table set, one of many representative works of the Bauhaus. To lower material costs, he used pipe with thicker walls but smaller diameter to fortify the cantilevered chair. Because of MUJI's concern for the environment, we have finished the piece with simple coating, rather than the original chrome plating.

Knowing that even masterpieces won't sell if the price is too high, MUJI isn't afraid to work to lower the price of an object that it deems to be of masterpiece quality. MUJI calls this appropriate pricing, or just pricing. Some of the tactics MUJI will take to make a justly priced masterpiece are trying different ways to procure materials, buying materials directly from the source, and educating suppli-ers—all in the hopes of hearing a customer exclaim, "What a great buy!" Instead of jacking up the price with brand identity, MUJI aims to make genuine products with the quality and materials of top brands and offer them to people at appropriate pric-es. There are several brands and manufacturers who could collaborate with MUJI to imbue popular products with advanced techniques and good quality. And there are many other brands out there that might share ideologies with MUJI, allowing our sales concept to not only be to develop new products, but to find MUJI-like prod-ucts from around the world. At the same time, nothing binds MUJI to produce new items every year just to revitalize the market. If we have a good product, we intend to keep selling it. It's this position that makes possible collaborations with a number of excellent brands and manufacturers, and allows us to circulate throughout the world a universal production experience called MUJI.

Right: Thonet No. 14 Chair, 19th Century.
Left: Beech Bentwood Chair with Wooden Seat, 2009.

Right: Chair No. 14, a masterpiece
by German furniture manufacturer Thonet.
Left: MUJI No. 14, which reinterprets
the charm of the original Chair No. 14
into a simpler and more everyday piece.

Beech Table, 2009.

The back of the chair becomes
one with the tabletop.

Beech Bentwood Chair with Wooden Seat, 2009.

Thonet's bentwood technique brings out the natural tendency
for wood to warp. There is something beautiful
about the smoothly flowing curves that result.

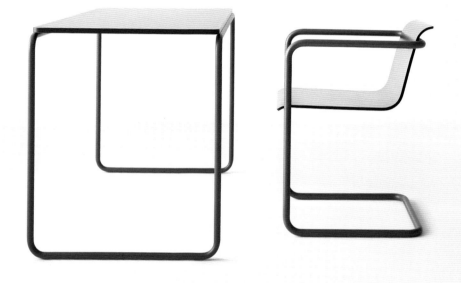

Tubular Steel Chair
Tubular Steel Desk, 2009.

An extremely simple cantilevered
chair and desk are derived from Bauhaus ideology.

Tubular Steel Low Table
Steel Shelf for Tubular Low Table, 2009.

It can be used as an audiovisual stand as well.
Its durability comes from the Thonet technique
that creates beautiful curves from tubes rolled
from steel plate only 2.5mm thick.

4 Identity and Communication of MUJI

Kenya HARA | Art Director

Nothing, Yet Everything

MUJI is an empty vessel. Its products fit into the context of every lifestyle, regardless of whether the person is old or young, male or female. MUJI does not design a table for young people and another table for couples in their sixties. The essence of MUJI's spirit is its ability to create one simple table about which many different people can say, "this table suits my lifestyle." Its essence lies in acceptance, not assertion. The functions of a MUJI product are not scrupulously laid out for the user. Instead, the product functions when acted upon by the user's intention and purpose. Some people call this "no design," but MUJI is not "no design." MUJI aims for de-

"Horizon" Campaign, Uyuni Salt Flats, Bolivia,
poster, 2003.

sign with such thoroughly considered receptivity that the product can both fit itself
as closely as possible to the user's intention, and adjust to any circumstance.

There is a traditional Japanese aesthetic that sees the utmost richness in what
is extremely plain. This plainness is different from the Western notion of simplicity. If
we define "simple" in the West as something that stems from a rational alignment of
purpose and use, then perhaps "emptiness" is the right word for extreme plainness.
It is an infinite flexibility that accepts each and every concept and adjusts to any purpose. This concept of "emptiness" lies at the center of the tea ceremony, *ikebana*, Noh
Theater, Japanese gardens and architecture, and all the other cultural practices that
emanate from uniquely Japanese aesthetics. The same is true of MUJI.

MUJI also aims for emptiness in its communication. MUJI is not the

message; the message must be an empty vessel able to receive whatever vision the customer has in mind. We measure the communication's success not by how well a message was conveyed, but by how many different images it was able to accept.

MUJI's customers interpret MUJI in different ways. Some think of MUJI as an urban refinement, while others think it's about ecology. Some see MUJI as an affordable brand. Others think of it as a reflection of Zen ideology. Some appreciate MUJI's relaxed, moderate design, and others see MUJI as "products without color." MUJI's advertising communication does not support any one of these interpretations, but allows for all of them to exist equally.

Just as football players rely on wordless communication and a thoughtful and reciprocal relationship to convey their next move, the most important role of

無印良品

"Horizon" Campaign, Mongolia,
poster, 2003.

advertising is making this kind of "eye contact" with customers. MUJI's ads act as empty vessels, accepting the interpretations of a variety of people and supporting these equally various expectations.

The image on the previous page is of the horizon on the salt flats in Uyuni, Bolivia, and the visual on this page is the horizon on the prairies of Mongolia. In a quest for the perfect image of "emptiness," I joined the photographer at both locations. These are extreme visions of earth and mankind; there is nothing, yet at the same time there is everything.

On the other hand, MUJI announces its vision in a newspaper ad once a year. Intended for both MUJI customers and employees, the ads summarize and store occasional thoughts on MUJI. On the following pages are English translations.

Identity and Communication of MUJI | Kenya HARA

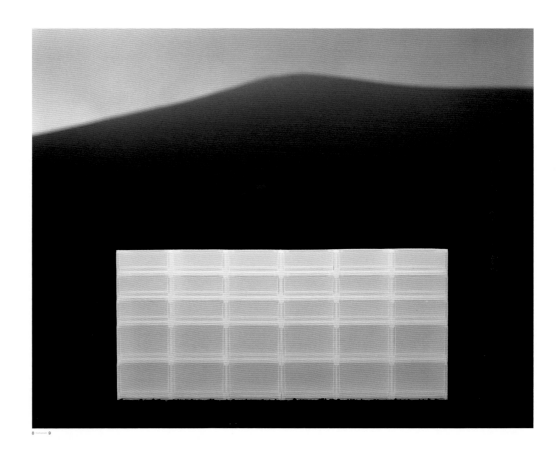

8 —— 9

10 —— 11

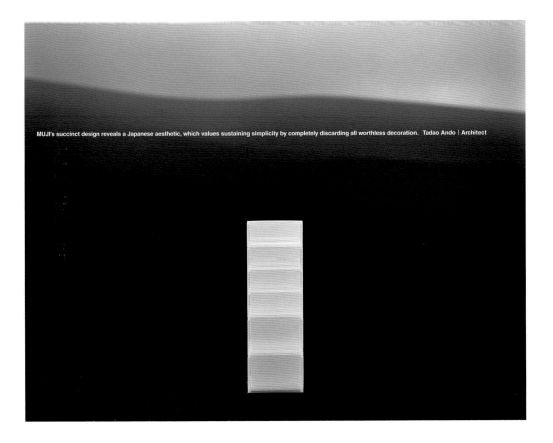

MUJI's succinct design reveals a Japanese aesthetic, which values sustaining simplicity by completely discarding all worthless decoration.   Tadao Ando │ Architect

"MUJI Milano Salone."
concept book, 2003.

It is the Most Universal Japanese Idea.   Shigeru Ban │ Architect

Identity and Communication of MUJI │ Kenya HARA

In the past, simple, succinct design has influenced our five senses as much as has elaborate design. This will remain true in the future.   Hiroshi Kashiwagi : Design critic

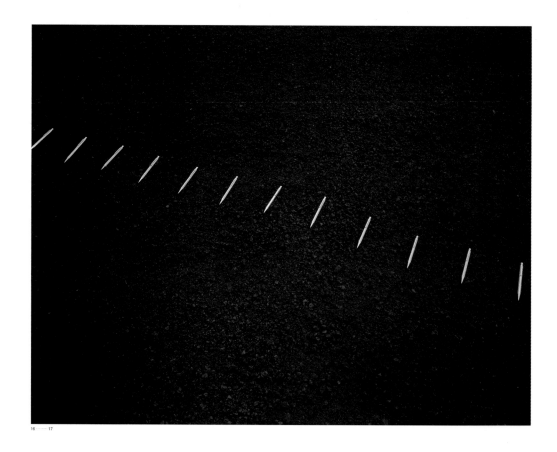

ISSEY MIYAKE, COMME des GARCONS, Yohji Yamamoto, and MUJI:
In Japan we alone speak the universal tongue of sensibilities. We must carry on.   Yohji Yamamoto | Fashion designer

MUJI is good for you! Jasper Morrison | Product designer

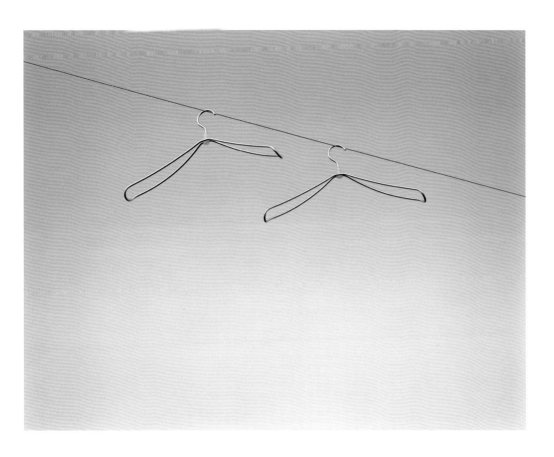

MUJI is an enormously large, empty vessel that accepts the sensitivities of anyone and everyone.   Kenya Hara | Graphic designer

Identity and Communication of MUJI | Kenya HARA

せません。無印良品は地球規模の消費の未来を見すえ

という理性的な満足感をお客さまに持っていただくこ

しかしながら「が」にも「で」にもレベルがあります。無印良品

多くの人々が指摘している通り、地球と人類の未来

一九八〇年に誕生した無印良品は、当初よりこうし

このような商品を生活のさまざまな局面で提供し続

る視点から商品づくりの本質を見すえ

という強い嗜好性を誘う商品づくりではありません。それは「これ

とが無印良品のヴィジョンです。これを目

標に、約五〇〇〇アイテムにのぼる商品を徹底して磨

しかしそのすべてに向き合って無印良品は存在して

無印良品

無印良品の未来

"Horizon" Campaign,
Uyuni Salt Flats, Bolivia,
newspaper ad, 2003.

The Future and MUJI

We make MUJI products look straight into the future of consumption on a global scale. We do not make objects to attract consumers who will say, "this is what I really want," or "I must have this." MUJI tries to attract not the customer who says "This is what I want," but rather the one who says, rationally, "this will do." MUJI doesn't "cater to appetite", but rather "applies to need." "Appetite" favors egoism and dissent. Within "applicability," on the other hand, a rational mind yields moderation and concession. At the same time, applicability may demand reconciliation or impose a touch of dissatisfaction on the customer. Even in applicability, levels are implied. MUJI aims for the highest level. In this context, raising the level of applicability means lowering the extent of the reconciliation and/or discontent of the consumer. MUJI aims to create a dimension of applicability that allows a consumer to say, with complete confidence, "this will do." "Appetite" favors egoism and dissent. Within "applicability," on the other hand, a rational mind yields moderation and concession. At the same time, applicability may demand reconciliation or impose a touch of dissatisfaction on the customer.

Even in applicability, levels are implied. MUJI aims for the highest level. In this context, raising the level of applicability means lowering the extent of the reconciliation and/or discontent of the consumer. MUJI aims to create a dimension of applicability that allows a consumer to say, with complete confidence, "this will do." This is what MUJI envisions. To achieve this goal, we will analyze and refine the more than 5,000 MUJI products in existence, thus realizing a new level of quality.

MUJI products are succinct. MUJI is manufactured through extremely rationalized processes, and MUJI is simple, but MUJI is not simple for the sake of minimalism as a style. MUJI is like an empty vessel. Simplicity and emptiness yield an absolute universality, so there is room within MUJI for any and all thoughts and opinions. MUJI has been called many things: low-consumption, inexpensive, simple, anonymous, natural. In our vision, MUJI is defined by none of these adjectives alone, but is in accordance with them all.

Recently many have noted the precarious position of mankind. We human beings are past the point of brainwashing one another, and are now enlightening one another as to our grave situation: we are casting a shadow on the future of the earth and of humankind. Now we are actively searching for more viable solutions and ways to carry them out in our daily life. The cultural collisions we witness around the world verify the exasperating limitations of the conventional pursuit of profit (as guaranteed in a free economy system). These collisions also prove that asserting individual cultural identities threatens the possibilities of global co-existence. We must topple the monopoly on profit and on individual cultural values, and practice rationality. We must restrain ourselves from self-assertive, egoistical ways. We must maintain a panoramic view of the world, and act in accordance, always. Unless we resort to a sense of value informed by this panoramic view, the world will find itself at an impasse. Every one of our contemporaries has probably already embraced this vision, and is ready to practice moderation.

MUJI was established in 1980. Ever since, it has worked within the bosom of this recognition, and its framework will remain unchanged.

Today, we seem surrounded by merchandise that can be divided into two categories: branded, and cheap. Objects in the first category compete on the basis of idiosyncrasies, innovative materials and decorative elements. They create scarcity value by establishing significance as a brand, and attract huge numbers of consumers who praise pricey objects. The other category is filled with objects manufactured as cheaply as possible, in countries with the lowest production costs, using the most inexpensive materials and the simplest processes.

MUJI belongs to neither of these groups. In the beginning, we pursued the policy and goal of "no design." But we have learned that high quality products don't come from "no design" that slights creativity. From now on, by finding the most compatible material and form, and designing the most compatible production process, MUJI will aim for an ultimate design based on "simplicity." This is not the same as trying to simply produce things inexpensively. While employing as simple a production process as possible, we will use a better quality material and process technology under scrutiny. MUJI will realize the richest, smartest products at a reasonable price.

Like the compass, which always points due North, through its simple products MUJI will indicate the basis and universal nature of life.

Below:
"House" Campaign, Morocco,
poster, 2004.

茶室と無印良品

写真は国宝、慈照寺「東求堂」。茶室の源流であり、今日言われる「和室」のはじまりとなった空間です。通称銀閣寺の名で親しまれている慈照寺は、室町末期に、足利義政の別荘として建てられました。義政は応仁の乱という長い戦乱に嫌気がさして、将軍の地位を息子に譲り、京都の東の端で静かに書画や茶の湯などの趣味を深めていく暮らしを求めたのです。応仁の乱は日本の歴史を二分するような大きな戦乱でした。義政によって始められたこの東山文化を発端として、日本の文化は新しい局面を開いていくことになります。

「同仁斎」、そんな義政が多くの時間を過ごした書斎。書院造りと呼ばれるこの部屋には、明かりとりの障子の手前に、書き物をする張り出しがしつらえられています。障子を開けて見る庭の風景は、軽の掛け軸のよう。張台の脇からは、書籍や真具の類が置かれていました。ひさしが長く、深い陰翳を宿す東求堂に、障子ごしの光が差し込む風情、そして障子の格子や畳の縁などで生み出されるシンプルな構成は、まぎれもなく日本の空間のひとつの原形。

今日、同仁斎が国宝に指定されている理由もここにあります。この同仁斎で義政は茶を味わい、ひとり静かに心を遊ばせたのでしょう。義政の元を訪れたとされる侘び茶の開祖、珠光もおそらくはこの部屋を訪れたはずです。

茶の湯は、室町末期から桃山時代にかけて確立されていきました。それは、大陸文化の影響を離れ、侘びや簡素さに日本独自の価値を見い出す試みでした。茶祖、珠光は、豪華さや「唐物」を尊ぶ船来志向を捨てて、冷え、枯れたものの風情、すなわち「侘び」に美を見出しました。さらに武野紹鴎を経たひとつの「見立て」です。茶室と無印良品に思いをはせるひとつの「見立て」です。茶室と無印良品に思いを託すものの見方を探求します。やがて千利休「日本風」すなわち簡素な造形に複雑な人間の内面性を託すものの見方を探求します。やがて千利休によって、茶の空間や道具・作法はひとつの極みへと導かれていきます。簡素さと沈黙、シンプルだからこそ、そこに何かを見ようとするイメージを招き入れることができる。利休はものの見方の多様性のなかに造形やコミュニケーションの無辺の可能性を見立てていきました。

このような美意識の系譜は古田織部、小堀遠州など、後の時代の才能たちに引き継がれ、茶道とともに日常の道具として、そして「桂離宮」のような建築空間に息づいています。勿論、現代の日本にもそれは受け継がれており、簡素さの中に価値や美意識を見立てていく無印良品の思想の源流もここに見つけることができます。

写真の中央に鎮座している器は無印良品の白磁の茶碗。これは日本で生まれた美意識の始原に思いをはせるひとつの「見立て」です。茶室と無印良品の、時を経たコラボレーションとしてご覧ください。無印良品はシンプルですが、価格を安くするだけの簡略化ではありません。適切な素材と技術を用いて、誰にでも、そしてどこにでも用いることのできる自在性、つまり「見立て」によって無限の可能性を発揮できるもののあり方を目指しています。写真の茶碗も同様、伝統的な白磁の産地、長崎の波佐見で誕生した一連の和の器は、いずれも際だってシンプルですが、日本の今日の食生活を考えつく、あらゆる食卓への対応を考慮した果ての簡潔さを体現しています。

五〇〇〇品目にのぼる商品で現代の多様な暮らしを見ていていく無印良品は、その活動の延長線上に「住まい」の形を探し始めています。衣料品、生活雑貨、食品など、今日の生活に向き合う製品群はおのずと暮らしの生きる形を描きます。床や壁の材質、キッチンのあり方、収納の合理性、人それぞれの生活スタイルに対応できる寝室や居室の可能性を考えていくうちに、「家」というテーマが見えてきました。既にウサギ小屋と呼ばれた日本の住宅ですが、かつてはウサギ小屋「木の家」の販売も開始しています。かつて日本の住宅に恵まれない住まいの形が発見できるはずです。その原像は、おそらく茶室に見る簡潔さにあらゆるイマジネーションを受けとめられる簡潔さにあるのです。

現在、白磁の茶碗とともに広告で紹介している茶室は、慈照寺・東求堂「同仁斎」、大徳寺玉林院「霞床席」、同「蓑庵」、大徳寺孤篷庵「直入軒」、同「山雲床」、武者小路千家「官休庵」。これらの空間は二〇〇五年のはじまりに、あらためて無印良品が向き合います。

無印良品

www.muji.net

MUJI and the Teahouse

Shown in the photograph is the origin of both the teahouse and the space considered a traditional Japanese-style room. It is Dojinsai, the four-and-a-half mat room of Togudo, in Kyoto's Jisho-ji. Also known as The Silver Pavillon, Jisho-ji was built as a villa for the Shogun Yoshimasa Ashikaga at the end of the 15th century. Tired of the long-running civil war (Onin-no-ran), Yoshimasa made his son Shogun and pursued a quiet life at Kyoto's east end, cultivating his taste for calligraphy and the tea ceremony. Although this long and wide-ranging conflict marked an historical turning point, new aspects of Japan's culture were initiated, based on the "eastern" culture Yoshimasa had begun to develop.

Yoshimasa spent a lot of time in Dojinsai, which was a study of sorts. In this *shoin* style room, before the translucent *shoji* doors, stands a long writing platform. When the *shoji* are open, the garden scenery evolves like a picture scroll. The staggered shelves hold books and tools. The deep eaves gracing Togudo with subtle shade, the light streaming through the *shoji*, the *shoji* latticework and the edges of the *tatami* mats; all affect a simple composition revealing the origins of Japanese space. This is one reason Dojinsai is a national treasure. Here Yoshimasa sipped tea and relaxed in tranquility. Murata Shuko, the founder of the tea ceremony, communed with Yoshimasa through tea and probably visited him here.

The tea ceremony was established during the Muromachi and Momoyama periods. It was an attempt to escape the influence of Continental (Chinese) culture and discover unique Japanese values within simplicity and *wabi* (austere beauty, elegant rusticity). Shuko rejected the imported tendency toward extravagance and Continental goods and discovered instead an aesthetic within *wabi*. Joou Takeno, a philosophical successor, advanced the quest for a uniquely Japanese perception, in which a simple form expresses the complexities of human nature. Influenced by Sen-no-Rikyu, both utensils and manners of the tea ceremony were pushed to the extreme: profound simplicity and silence. This very simplicity invites imagination. Rikyu discerned the infinite possibilities of form and communication in the multiplicity of perspectives.

The legacy of this aesthetic was passed on to gifted individuals of later generations such as Oribe Furuta and Enshu Kobori, and still lives on in the tea ceremony, everyday tools, and architectural spaces like Katsura Imperial Villa. Contemporary Japan has inherited the concept of discernment (*mitate*), whence originates MUJI's ideology, which perceives value and beauty within simplicity.

The white porcelain bowl at the center of the photo is a MUJI rice bowl, another example of *mitate*, the judgment that drives thought about the origin of Japanese aesthetics. The photo illustrates collaboration between a tearoom and *Mujirushi Ryohin* that transcends time.

MUJI is simple, but it simplifies not only to lower prices. MUJI uses appropriate materials and techniques and aims for a way for things to exist that can demonstrate infinite possibilities through *mitate*, or the ability to adjust to use by anyone, in any circumstance. The rice bowl in the photo has this quality. These bowls are produced for MUJI in the town of Hasami in Nagasaki Prefecture, Japan's traditional porcelain production center. They are strikingly simple, but have the kind of simplicity that represents not only scrutiny of today's dietary culture, but also consideration of all sorts of dining situations.

MUJI offers over five thousand items that adapt to a variety of contemporary lifestyles and has extended its program to include a form of housing: the spaces in which we conduct our lives. Products for daily living such as clothing, household goods and food naturally depict the contours of a lifestyle. As MUJI considered materials for flooring and walls, the proper appointment of a kitchen, storage solutions and the possibilities for bedrooms and living rooms compatible with anyone's personal lifestyle, the theme "house" came to the forefront. Sales of MUJI's "Wood House" are proceeding apace. Limitations on resources and materials that gave rise to the term "rabbit hutches" actually give MUJI the opportunity to discover housing options that fully utilize these shortages.

We're likely to see the ideal form of this kind of living in Japanese teahouses, with their simplicity and the freedom from specifics, which allows an infinite variety of interpretations and imagination.

The following teahouses and studies can be found in current MUJI ads, each photographed with a white porcelain MUJI rice bowl: The Togudo Dojinsai; Kasumidokoseki and Sa-an (teahouses in Gyokurin-in, Kyoto's Daitoku-ji); Jikinyuken study and Sanunjo (teahouse in Koho-an, Daitoku-ji); and Kankyu-an (teahouse in the Mushakouji-Senke tea school).

"Teahouse" Campaign,
newspaper ad, 2005.

Above: Dojinsai study in Togudo Hall, Kyoto's Jisho-ji temple
(The Silver Pavillion) and the adjoining garden, Ginshadan.
Below: Kasumidokoseki teahouse at Gyokurin-in,
Kyoto's Daitoku-ji (temple).

無印良品

"Teahouse" Campaign,
posters, 2005.

無印良品

Identity and Communication of MUJI | Kenya HARA

身近な光景に眼をこらします。

用いられているタモ材は、バットやラケットなどに利用されている硬くて粘りのある素材、つまり丈夫でしなやかな木材です。「タモ」という名の由来は、北陸地方で田んぼのあぜに植えられていたため「田面（たも）」の木と呼ばれていたため、力を加えても折れずによく「たわむ」ところからきたという説などがあります。いずれもはるか昔から日本人の身近な木であったことがうかがわれます。時がたっても変化の少ない落ち着いた色調や、節目の少ないまっすぐにのびた木目には端正な味わいと安心感があります。家具に最も適した素材を探していくうちに、おのずとタモにたどり着きました。

無印良品の製品には、個性の強い形の主張がありません。シンプルに仕上げられたそれらは一見単調に見えるかもしれません。けれどもそこには、目には見えない暮らしの心地よさを探りあてていく冷静な工夫の積み重ねがあります。歴史や風土の中で道具として形をなしていった知恵のあり方を、かつては「ノーデザイン」と呼んだこともありました。しかし現在、無印良品はここに「デザイン」の本質があると考えています。

今日、無印良品のデザインは世界で高い評価をいただくようになりました。世界のプロダクトデザインが一堂に会する二〇〇五年のドイツ iF 賞においては五つの金賞を同時に受賞しました。ラジオ付きCDプレーヤー、DVDプレーヤー、シュレッダー、電話機、角形紙筒ラックがその受賞の対象でした。これらベーシックな製品に対する受賞によって無印良品のものづくりは大きな自信と勇気をいただくことができました。現在、私たちはそれをはっきりと「デザイン」と呼び、その品質を向上させるために、世界中のデザイナーたちと連携しています。

無印良品のデザインは、流行や時代の気分ではありません。若さや老いもターゲットにはしません。テクノロジーの先端に必要以上に意識を尖らせることもありません。基本は人への興味です。今日の地球で働き、憩う人々への興味です。身の丈にあった住まいを作り、安全なものを食べ、眠り、時には旅をし、笑いや涙に包まれる普通の人々。そういう人々の暮らしがもう少し幸福になるためのお手伝いを、六〇〇〇を超える製品を通して続けていくことが無印良品の役割です。資本の論理よりも人間の論理が少しだけまさっている点が私たちのオリジナリティです。

本年の無印良品の広告は商品に重点を置きます。きちんとおすすめできる製品をひとつずつご紹介していく予定です。タモ材の家具をはじめ、独創的なウレタン成型による「ふっくら成型ソファ」、操作が簡単で存在感をそのまま「壁掛式CDプレーヤー」、駅や公園にある時計をそのまま「掛時計・腕時計・置時計」にした明快なラインナップ、流れるようにきれいなアルミ製のシェードを持つ「アームライト」、どんな食卓にも素直になじむ「和の器・洋の器」シリーズなどなど、ひとつひとつの製品を通して皆様に「なるほど」と無印良品の成長をご理解いただきたいと考えています。

人と人、そして生活を冷静に観察したら……厳選な素材と技術を組み合わせたら……質を落とさず低コストをつきつめたら……自然や環境に配慮したら……お客さまの声に耳を傾けていったら……世界中のデザイナーと連携をしていったら……無印良品のデザインは、しぜんとこうなりました。

ぜんとこうなりました

無印良品

写真は無印良品のタモ材のベッドと椅子です。
背もたれの角度が同じに設計されているので横
から眺めるとふたつの背のラインがぴったりと
一致します。同じ「背もたれ」に無理のない形を
探っていくうちに、しぜんとこうなりました。
寝室でベッドに寄り添う椅子の情景をご想像く
ださい。決して特別なことではありません。むしろ
きわめてよくある日常のシーン。家具は先端に向

"What Happens Naturally" Campaign,
newspaper ad, 2006.

What Happens Naturally

In this photo are the MUJI bed and chair. Because the backrests are designed to have the same angle, when the pieces are viewed from the side, the backs align perfectly. Our mission was to create a reasonable, genuinely modest form. This is what happened naturally.

Picture, if you will, a bedroom. Beside the bed stands a chair. There is nothing special about the image. In fact, the scene is quite ordinary. Furniture tapers off at the head. The inconspicuous fusion of the reclining lines creates a spot of comforting harmony. MUJI ponders scenes like these, moments of everyday life.

The MUJI bed and the MUJI chair are both made of tamo, a variation of Manchurian ash. Used for baseball bats and tennis rackets, tamo is solid and pliable. The name tamo could come from the fact that in Japan's Hokuriku district, along the Sea of Japan, it often grew between rice paddies: tamo. Or perhaps tamo comes from tawamu, to bend without breaking. Either way, it's clear that tamo has been a familiar material to the Japanese since ancient times. The unchanging and sober color of the wood, along with its straight-growing grain, burled only slightly, diffuse a sense of tenderness, and a feeling of security. Looking for the perfect wood for our furniture, we came upon tamo naturally.

Consider form; MUJI products do not make individualistic statements through their shapes. Objects that are made simply may at first appear monotonous. However, in their accumulation of calmly determined design choices are discovered the invisible comforts of daily life. This is a wisdom that, within the context of history or environment, is transformed into tools. Once, we called this "non-design". But today MUJI recognizes that this is in fact the essence of design.

MUJI's design is internationally recognized and highly accredited around the world. At the 2005 iF International Forum Design competition, we won five golds in product design: for our DVD player, shredder, telephone, CD player with radio, and our square paper tube rack system. Winning awards for basic products like these gave us tremendous confidence and courage in regard to "making things". Now we proudly call this "design", and in the interest of improving the quality of our products, are collaborating with designers around the world.

The wellspring of MUJI design has nothing to do with fashion or the mood of the day. Our target is neither youth nor age. We don't pay any more attention than necessary to leading technology. The ethos of MUJI is interest in people. Our concern is for those who work and rest sharing the planet of today: people who create their living spaces with realistic expectations, have fun with their attire, eat safe food, sleep, go on a trip now and then, are enveloped by the usual ups and downs, laughter and tears: ordinary people. MUJI's role, accomplished through more than 6,000 MUJI products, is to continue to help people have a life that's a little happier each day. Our originality comes from the fact that in our work, the logic of capitalism is surpassed slightly by that of humanity.

Coolly observing people among people, and life,
Integrating optimal materials and technologies,
Investigating low cost while maintaining high quality,
Considering nature and the environment,
Listening to the voices of our customers,
Working with the world's designers,
This is what happens naturally.

手は美しい。よく働く手には思わず見とれてし
まいます。派手な装飾などしない指先こそきれい
だと感じている人は少なくないはずです。素肌や
素手がきれいであることをうれしく思う気持ちは、
天然素材の安心感や、洗いたてのシーツを心地よく
感じる気分と似ていないでしょうか。

日本では、玄関で靴をぬいで家に上がります。
その結果すばらしく清潔な生活空間が手に入り
ます。また、公共空間はとりわけ清潔です。空港の
床やオフィスのロビーなどには、寝転がれるくらい
きれいな場所もあるほど。海外から帰ると、凹凸
が少ない道路を、振動の少ないクルマで静かに走
る心地よさが、日本独特であることに気づきます。
清潔な空間や隅々まで気を行き届かせる配慮。そこ
に価値をおく文化が私たちの文化なのです。

たとえば、仕事をするということは、誰かの指図
に従って動くということではなく、主体的に価値
ある作業を積み重ねること。掃除をする人も、工事
をする人も、料理を作る人も、なすべき仕事を完遂
するという暗黙の精神をたずさえて働いています。
時間が来たから掃いたり拭いたり、そろえたり。
といって作業を放り出したりはしません。だから
日本から生まれるものや空間は、やさしくてきれい
なのです。

一四〇年ほど前に、西洋の文化を受け入れるこ
とによって日本の文化は混沌に直面しました。今
でもその大きな混乱は続いています。ですから私
たちのまわりの環境は、必ずしも理想的な状況と
は言えない矛盾に満ちています。また、アジアにお
ける経済の爆発と、低コストを求める競争によって
生活文化の質はさらに混迷の度を深めているかも
しれません。そうであればこそ、私たちは繊細で、
簡素で、丁寧で、清潔な自分たちの文化の中に確
かにある美意識を「資源」として再確認する必要
があるのです。

無印良品は二〇〇七年の末、ニューヨークに北米
一号店を開きました。特別な店舗ではなく普通の
無印良品です。さしたる宣伝も行なっていません
が、現地では大きな反響を生み、好意を持って迎
えられました。無印良品としては喜ばしいことで
すが、評価は単に無印良品だけではなく、その背
後にも向けられています。普通の無印良品やその
製品が世界の人々に注目される理由は、私たちの
暮らしの基本、つまり簡素ながら配慮のゆきとど
いた日本の美意識が、世界の人々に共感されはじ
めているからです。

世界の人々は今、気づきはじめています。安く
生産され、形だけのブランディングで味付けされ
たものを手にしても幸せにはなれないことを。古
くからの産地の手にする人に、使いやすさが伝わり
ます。それを手にする人に、使いやすさが伝わり
ます。生活文化の中に審まられてきた美意識が、
ものや作法に宿っているから、人はそこに豊かさ
を読み取り、充実や幸福を感じるのです。

無印良品は単なる製品の集まりではありません。
それらは生活の隅々までじっくり考え抜いた気配
りの集合体。本当に大事なことを簡潔にやさしく
体現したいと考えています。厳しさが続く世界だ
からこそ丁寧に、そしてやさしく。

138 ——— 139

やさしくしよう

無印良品

"Let's Take Care" Campaign,
newspaper ad, 2008.

Let's Take Care

Hands are beautiful. We're subconsciously drawn to active, hard-working hands. We expect that those who find plain, clean fingers beautiful outnumber those who are attracted to elaborately ornamented ones. The pleasure we get out of clean hands and skin must be similar to the security and comfort we enjoy in natural materials or freshly washed sheets.

In Japan, shoes come off as soon as the house is entered, resulting in exceptionally clean living spaces. Public spaces, too, are particularly clean. There are even floors in airports or lobbies in office buildings that are kept so clean that you feel like just laying down. Returning to Japan from abroad, you might rediscover the uniqueness of cozy rides in smoothly running cars on even pavement. In this experience, you recognize a unique trait of Japan; the care that extends to every detail of our environment.

Take work for example. It might be said that in Japan, to work means not to serve under someone but to accumulate actions that are worthy according to one's own standards. No matter the occupation, whether cleaning, construction, cooking or any other, Japanese practice their trade according to a kind of unspoken ethos to accomplish what needs to be done. Sweeping, wiping down, and straightening up: a job is finished when everything is tidy. A job is not left half-done just because the clock shows the end of the workday. This explains why objects originating in Japan and spaces created there are gently welcoming and beautiful.

About 140 years ago, Japan admitted an influx of Western culture and found itself facing confusion. A great disorder remains. Our surroundings are far from ideal; they are full of contradictions. It could be that the deepening disarray of the culture of our daily lives is due to the economic surge in the rest of Asia and the fierce competition for cheap production. If that's the case, we Japanese must reconfirm as a true resource the aesthetic sense so present in our culture of sensitivity, simplicity, care and cleanliness.

MUJI opened its first US branch in New York at the end of 2007. This was no special store, just an ordinary MUJI shop. Despite the fact that we didn't launch a huge ad campaign to coincide with the opening, we garnered a huge response and were welcomed with open arms. For MUJI of course this was fortunate, but we found that the people were interested not only in our products, but also in what's behind them. It seems that ordinary MUJI shops and products attract worldwide attention because they embody Japanese aesthetics, or the foundation of our lifestyle, which values simplicity and compassion, and people around the world have begun to experience a certain empathy for those aesthetics and the values that give rise to them.

Today the world has begun to recognize that products that are premised on low-cost manufacturing and flavored with token branding can't make us happy. People feel the serviceability, the user-friendliness, of things that are created over time in an established production locale. Because the aesthetic nurtured in a particular daily culture lives on in its objects and manners, people recognize in those a true luxury, and feel happy and content.

MUJI's products are not a mere assemblage of objects. They are an aggregate of intense consideration of the entirety of living. We aim to materialize what is truly significant and meaningful to human life in a simple yet sensitive way. Even more so because the trouble in this world is not going to subside, MUJI will continue to be careful and sensitive.

やさしくしよう
無印良品

やさしくしよう
無印良品

"Let's Take Care" Campaign,
posters, 2008.

Identity and Communication of MUJI | Kenya HARA

ニューヨークのセントラルパーク、午後三時。十日前に生まれたばかりという娘を抱いたお母さんとお祖母さんが、薄日のさすベンチに腰掛けてのんびりしたひとときを過ごしています。世界は今、大不況の嵐が吹き荒れていますが、人間の幸福のかたちは、景気の良し悪しにかかわらず、変わらない普遍としてそこにありました。

四〇丁目には、ニューヨークタイムズの本社ビルが、真新しい姿を見せています。建築家レンゾ・ピアノの設計による美しい高層ビルは、新しいニューヨークのランドマーク。このビルの一階に無印良品ニューヨーク三号店が誕生しています。すでにMoMAのミュージアムショップの中で親しまれてきた無印良品は、一昨年のSOHOの一号店、そして最新のチェルシー三号店とともに、すっかりニューヨークの街になじんできました。しかしながら、通りからながめる無印良品のお店は、日本のそれと全く同じ。どこに行っても、変わらないペースで、簡素の美を、静かに謳いあげています。

ニューヨーク、イスタンブール、ローマ、北京。二〇〇八年に無印良品はこれらの都市に新しいお店を出しました。世界のメトロポリス、ニューヨーク。かつては東ローマ帝国の首都コンスタンティノープルとして、またオスマントルコの首都として約千五百年の長きにわたってローマに次いで世界の中心として君臨した都イスタンブール。そしてまさに世界文明の中枢をつくったローマ。さらには、今後の世界文明の新機軸を担おうとする北京。この四都市に、無印良品はくしくも同じ年に出店を果たしました。アジアの東の端の文化と美意識がこうして世界へと還流している情景には、とても深い感慨と、胸の高鳴る誇らしさを覚えます。そのいずれの都市でも、無印良品は、すでになくてはならない存在として、それぞれの土地の人々の意識や暮らしに溶け込んでいるのです。まるで水のように。

無理をしないこと。背伸びをしないこと、暮らしの工夫を積み重ね、無駄を省き、低価格を目指すこと。しかしそれでも豪華さやパワーブランドに一歩も引けを取らない簡素の美を求め続けること。

無印良品は水のようでありたいと思います。水は穏やかで、不可欠で、いつも人の傍らにあり、想いと潤いを提供します。酒のような華やかさはなく、香水のように人々を魅了することはありませんが、純粋であり続けることで、全ての人々の普通の健やかさを保証し続けます。穏やかな水は、年月を重ねることで、山をも削り、時には大きな自然の力の現れとして岩をも砕く力を発揮します。その隅々へ、人々の求める場所に、広がって行きたいと考えています。

世界は今、低調な経済の話題の中に沈み込んでいますが、しかしこういう時にこそ、基本と普遍を丁寧に見つめ直し、一人でも多くの方々の暮らしに寄り添うことができればと願っています。どうか安心して、ゆっくりしたペースでいきませんか。無印良品はいつも水のように、あなたの暮らしを応援しています。

水のようでありたい

無印良品

Like Water

It's three o'clock in the afternoon in New York's Central Park. The sun sheds soft beams on a woman cradling her infant; she spends a relaxed moment on a bench with her mother, the new child's grandmother. The world is gripped by a storm we call economic recession, and yet on this park bench we find a human happiness that is universal and everlasting, insusceptible to swings in the economy.

Soaring over 40th street is the brand-new building of The New York Times. Designed by Renzo Piano, it is a fresh New York landmark. MUJI's flagship New York shop is on the first floor of this beautiful structure.

Americans and MUJI products first became acquainted in the MoMA store in the Museum of Modern Art. In 2007, MUJI opened its own first shop in SoHo, and our third shop opened recently in Chelsea, making MUJI a familiar icon to New Yorkers. Still, from the street, our New York stores look exactly like their counterparts in Japan. Wherever it stands, MUJI continues to celebrate the aesthetics of simplicity, quietly, directly, and at its own pace.

New York, Istanbul, Rome, Beijing. In 2008, MUJI opened flagships in all of these cities. New York: the world's metropolis. Istanbul, historically known as Constantinople: once the capital of the Eastern Roman Empire, and later, of the Ottoman Empire, which controlled the world and marked its center for a millennium and a half. Rome: the nucleus of world civilization. Beijing: expected to shoulder the milestones of global culture in the new era. Curiously, MUJI opened branches in all four of these grand cities in the same year. Seeing this diffusion of the culture and aesthetics from the Eastern tip of Asia to the rest of the world fills us with great satisfaction. In each and every one of these metropolitan communities, MUJI has become part and parcel of the lifestyles and consciousness of its people, a modest and yet indispensable presence—like water.

Not shooting for the moon. Not trying to do more than we are able. Adding solution to solution for better living, cutting waste and aiming for lower prices. Yet still continually pursuing the beauty of simplicity while holding the field against luxury and power brands. These are MUJI's principles.

We want to be just like water. Water is calm, essential, always nearby, giving us rest and richness. It has not the brilliance of liquor, nor does it attract us like perfume, but pure and constant, it helps us maintain normal, natural health. Calm water wears away even mountains over many millions of years and sometimes exudes an erosive power strong enough to grind massive boulders into sand, manifesting itself as an immense mainspring of natural power. While holding close this kind of power, MUJI envisions spreading its wings calmly, soaring the skies of the globe, touching down wherever people wish it so.

Today our world is grappling with a global economic downturn. All the more so does MUJI yearn to embrace the daily lives of as many people as we comfortably can, by carefully reexamining basics and universality. Won't you join us in somehow relaxing and living life unhurried, at your own pace?

Like water, MUJI is always here, for your life.

Above:
"Like Water" Campaign, Istanbul, poster, 2009.
Below:
"Like Water" Campaign, Beijing, poster, 2009.

水のようでありたい

無印良品

pp 146-147
"Like Water" Campaign, Rome,
poster, 2009.

水のようでありたい

無印良品

pp 148-149
MUJI shopping bag.

The present brown kraft-paper
MUJI shopping bag is a result of
many detailed improvements over time.

The Face of MUJI

MUJI's tags and labels are simple expressions of the elimination of extras without leading to shabbiness, and are designed to make the customer feel a kind of pride in choosing the product.

What MUJI aims for is not, "this is what I really want," but rather, "this will do." Typical brands make the customer want to possess the brand, and induce a mentality that leads him to pay a high price—happily—to acquire it. MUJI is the exact opposite. There is a small egotism hidden in the "this is what I really want" mentality. MUJI would like to curb this egotism by bringing forth a new sense of consumer satisfaction within the logic of the constraint of excess implied by "this will do."

Here's an example of the kind of values that MUJI aims to cultivate: even a consumer with the flexibility afforded by much wealth would be both proud and happy to pass on purchasing a more ornate towel with elaborate details in order to choose a MUJI towel in whose material and form, which were carefully considered in terms of utility, there is neither excess nor deficiency.

MUJI's daily-use products need not be part of a complete collection. MUJI shows its true worth in the reality of a modest life that exists between one thing and another: things like a soap dispenser and a hanger; a storage box in a closet, invisible from the outside; a towel or slippers, sheets or pillowcases; file folders or notebooks. It's perfectly fine to have a luxurious sofa in the living room and to adorn oneself with clothing and bags from favorite brands. But a life completely buried in the insistence of brands is often stressful and strained. MUJI offers everyday goods that, like well-purified air, fill the space between those kinds of objects.

In this way, MUJI products must remain simple, while imparting purity like that of fresh air. The MUJI tags and labels are designed with this purpose. They express liberation from trends, polishing the ordinary with this great feeling of freshness. Their concise design utilizes beige (the color of unbleached paper), dark brownish red (the corporate color), and the extremely common Helvetica and similarly plain Japanese fonts.

Every label carries a few lines, called "reason text," explaining what points led to the product's development as part of the MUJI line. The tags and labels on every one of MUJI's 7,000 products are MUJI's face, and everything about them is controlled by an explicit system of design.

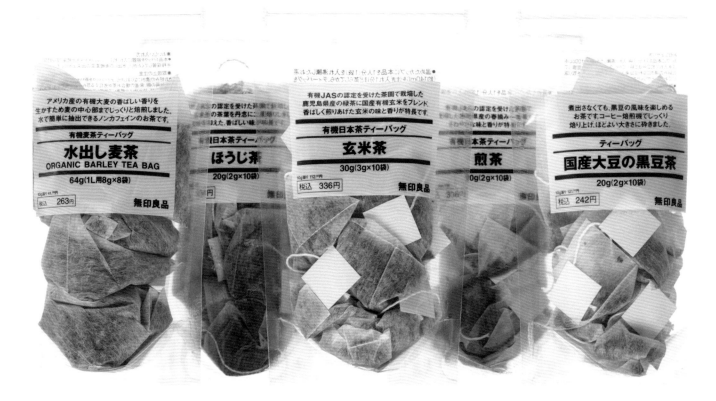

The face of MUJI. In the most minimal way,
MUJI packaging presents the unique qualities of each product,
creating a distinct identity.

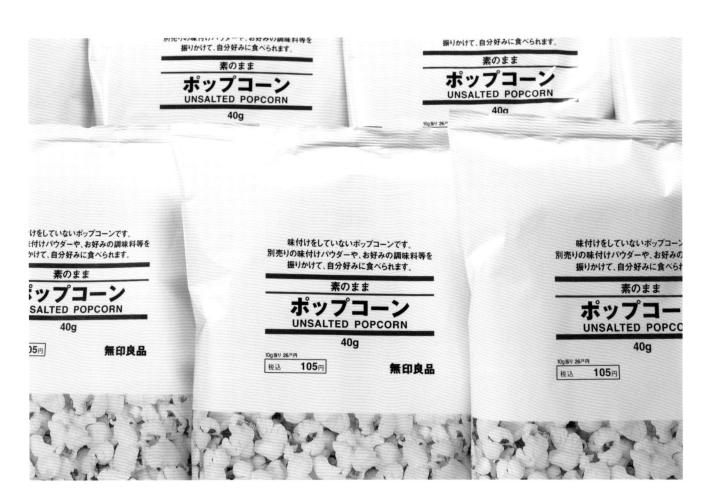

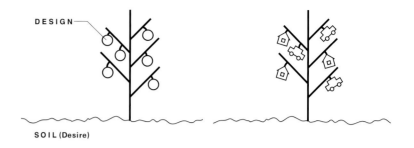

DESIGN

SOIL (Desire)

The Education of Desire

A product is like fruit growing on a tree. If you want to improve the quality of the fruit, or the product, you have to grow a healthy tree, and to do that you need to improve the condition of the soil in which it grows.

In this metaphor, the tree corresponds to a company, and the soil's condition corresponds to the level of desire of the people who make up the market on which the company builds its foundation. To understand that level, we have to ask ourselves, what do these people long for, as they go about their daily lives? What subconscious desires to they have? Within the answers to these questions, we uncover a new kind of marketing.

The tree, or company, absorbs people's desires and bears fruit, or products. This is why fertilizing the soil of desire is the most effective way to yield high-quality products. Design is not the process of polishing or decorating the fruit. In this macroscopic cycle, design must have some influence over the quality of desire.

MUJI's marketing is not about making products that respond generously to people's desires. It's about creating a new market by changing the quality of people's appetite for living, and influencing the shape their desires take. In other words, we intend to anticipate the future of consumption and generate a new level of desire in the world's consumption. MUJI's message is not the source of the education; instead, the individual who gets hold of a MUJI product personally awakens to the rational relationship that exists between manufacturing and consumption.

Given the simplicity of MUJI's products, it's not unusual for them to be copied. However, the strong feeling you sense when holding a MUJI product in your hand does not emanate solely from its extremely simplified form. There is a philosophy reflected in all of MUJI's products, communication, and design: a single, consistent ideology in seemingly simple and low-cost products. This cannot be copied easily.

Once a person buys a MUJI product and comes across the MUJI philosophy, it is our hope that he comes to a realization that buying an extravagant and overpriced object is not necessarily something to be proud of, and may in fact be a slightly foolish move. Thus begins a voluntary education of desire. From this experience onwards, the user cannot help but be aware of the straightforward appeal of MUJI's products. MUJI is like a mirror, reflecting the user's own potential. This is the kind of presence that MUJI's tags and packaging aim for.

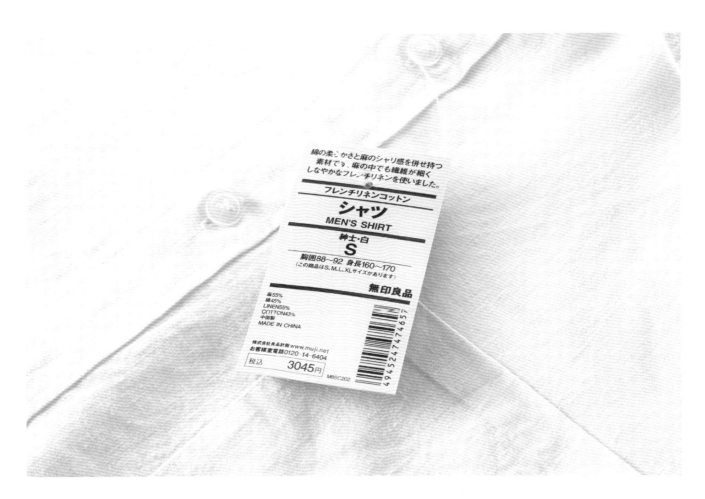

The reason for each item's existence is conveyed concisely on tags and labels. The subtle colors of the toiletry line employ a special simplicity, and create an overall unified balance.

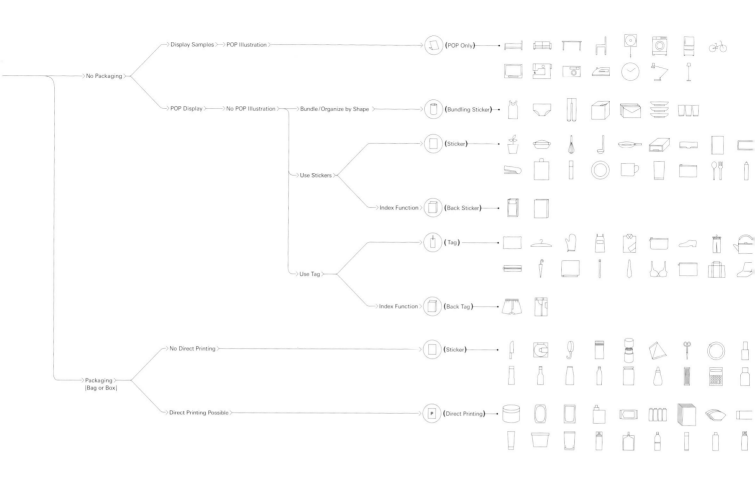

Above: A flow chart for the criteria that governs
decision-making about different types of packaging.

Below: The MUJI tagging system
All MUJI tags follow a clear set of rules.
Each tag includes an explanation of
why the item is a MUJI product.

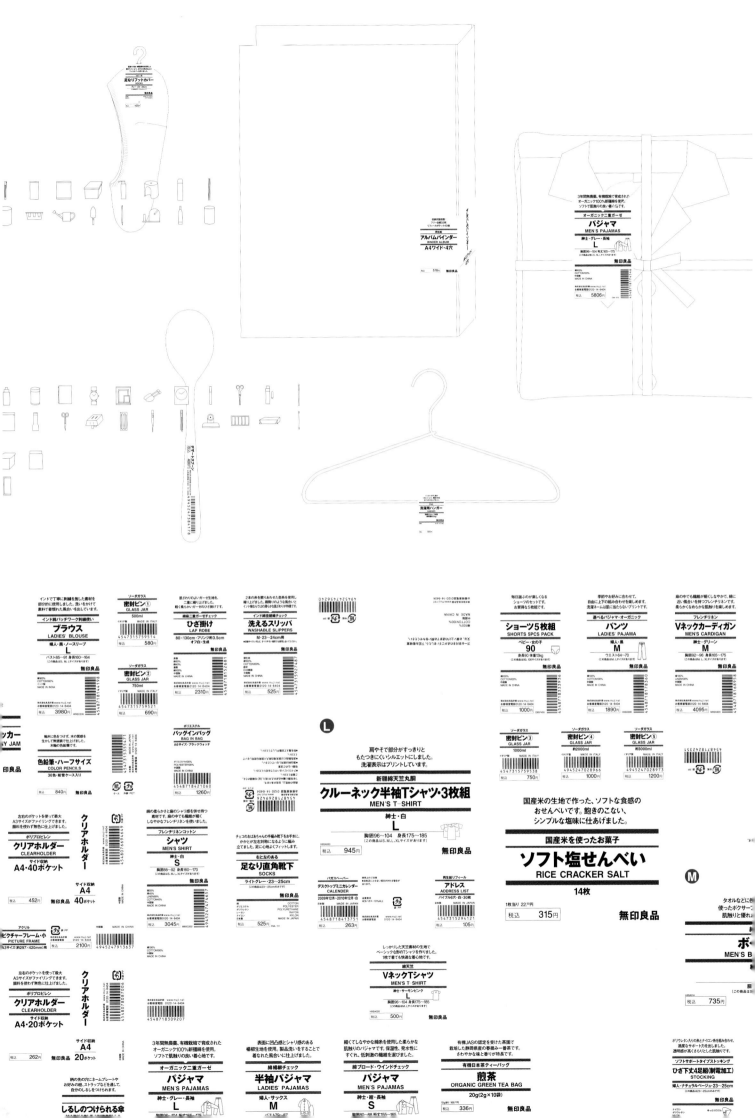

無印良品 商品ラベル

足なりリブフットカバー SOCKS グレー・23~25cm 無印良品

アルバムバインダー BINDER ALBUM A4ワイド・4穴 無印良品

オーガニックニ重ガーゼ
パジャマ MEN'S PAJAMAS
紳士・グレー・長袖
綿100% COTTON100% 中国製 MADE IN CHINA
5806円

洗濯用ハンガー HANGER 無印良品

インドで丁寧に刺繍を施した素材を部分的に使用しました。洗いをかけて素材を着慣れた風合いを出しています。
インド綿パッチワーク刺繍使い
ブラウス LADIES' BLOUSE
婦人・黒・ノースリーブ **L**
バスト85~91 身長160~164
(この商品はS、M、Lサイズがあります)
綿100% COTTON100% MADE IN INDIA
3980円

ソーダガラス **密封ビン①** GLASS JAR 500ml イタリア製 MADE IN ITALY 580円
ソーダガラス **密封ビン②** GLASS JAR 750ml イタリア製 MADE IN ITALY 690円

肌ざわりのよいガーゼ生地を二重に織り上げました。
綿四重ガーゼチェック
ひざ掛け LAP ROBE
80×130cm・フリンジ約3.5cm オフ白・生成
綿100% MADE IN CHINA
2310円

2本の糸を寄りあわせた密糸を使用し、織り上げました。細身のふっくら風合いとインド綿ならではの丈夫さが特徴です。
インド綿三重構造チェック
洗えるスリッパ WASHABLE SLIPPERS
M・23~24cm用
綿100% MADE IN CHINA
525円

毎日違った柄が楽しくなるショーツのセットです。お買得な5枚組です。
ショーツ5枚組 SHORTS 5PCS PACK
ベビー・女の子 **90**
身長90 体重13kg
(この商品は80、100サイズがあります)
綿100% 中国製 MADE IN CHINA
1000円

季節やお好みに合わせて、自由に上下の組み合わせを楽しめます。洗濯ネームは裏につけないプリントです。
選べるパジャマ・オーガニック
パンツ LADIES' PAJAMA
婦人・黒 **M**
ウエスト64~70
綿100% 中国製 MADE IN CHINA
1890円

麻の中でも繊細で肌ざわりのよい、絹に近い風合いをもつフレンチリネンです。柔らかくなめらかな肌触りが特徴です。
フレンチリネン
Vネックカーディガン MEN'S CARDIGAN
紳士・グリーン **M**
胸囲92~96 身長165~175
麻100% LINEN100% MADE IN CHINA
4095円

触れた色も守す、木の質感を生かして無塗装で仕上げました。木製の色鉛筆です。
色鉛筆・ハーフサイズ COLOR PENCILS
36色・紙管ケース入り
840円 無印良品

ポリエステル
バッグインバッグ BAG IN BAG
A6サイズ・ブラックウォッチ
ポリエステル100% POLYESTER100% MADE IN JAPAN
1260円

ソーダガラス **密封ビン③** GLASS JAR 1000ml イタリア製 MADE IN ITALY 750円
ソーダガラス **密封ビン④** GLASS JAR 約2000ml イタリア製 1000円
ソーダガラス **密封ビン⑤** GLASS JAR 約3000ml イタリア製 MADE IN ITALY 1200円

肩やそで部分がすっきりともたつきにくいシルエットにしました。洗濯表示はプリントしています。
新疆綿天竺丸胴
クルーネック半袖Tシャツ・3枚組 MEN'S T-SHIRT
紳士・白 **L**
胸囲96~104 身長175~185
(この商品はS、M、L、XLサイズがあります)
945円 無印良品

左右のポケットを使って最大A3サイズがファイリングできます。顔料を使わず無色に仕上げました。
ポリプロピレン
クリアホルダー CLEARHOLDER
サイド収納 A4・40ポケット
A4 40ポケット
452円

綿の柔らかさと麻のシャリ感を併せ持つ素材です。麻の中でも繊細で肌ざわりしなやかなフレンチリネンを使いました。
フレンチリネンコットン
シャツ MEN'S SHIRT
紳士・白 **S**
胸囲88~92 身長160~170
(この商品はS、M、L、XLサイズがあります)
3045円

チェコのおばあちゃんの手編み靴下をお手本に、かかとが左右対称になるよう編み立てました。足にぴったりフィットします。
右と左のある
足なり直角靴下 SOCKS
ライトグレー・23~25cm
(この商品は23~25cmのものです)
525円 無印良品

バガスペーパー
デスクトップミニカレンダー CALENDER
2009年12月~2010年12月・B6
263円

再生紙リフィール
アドレス ADDRESS LIST
バイブル6穴・B・30枚
105円

国産米の生地で作った、ソフトな食感のおせんべいです。飽きのこない、シンプルな塩味に仕上げました。
国産米を使ったお菓子
ソフト塩せんべい RICE CRACKER SALT
14枚
1枚当り 22.5円
315円 無印良品

アクリル
ピクチャーフレーム・小 PICTURE FRAME
A3サイズ(297×420mm)用
2100円

左右のポケットを使って最大A3サイズがファイリングできます。顔料を使わず無色に仕上げました。
ポリプロピレン
クリアホルダー CLEARHOLDER
サイド収納 A4・20ポケット
A4 20ポケット
262円 無印良品

しっかりした天竺素材の生地でベーシックな形のTシャツを作りました。1枚で着ても快適な着心地です。
綿天竺
VネックTシャツ MEN'S T-SHIRT
紳士・サーモンピンク **L**
胸囲96~104 身長175~185
(この商品はS、M、L、XLサイズがあります)
500円 無印良品

タオルなどに…使ったボクサー…肌触りと優れ…
ボ… MEN'S B…
735円

柄の先のパニネームプレートやお好みの組、ストラップなどに、自分のしるしをつけられる。
しるしのつけられる傘

3年間無農薬、有機栽培で育成されたオーガニック100%新疆綿を使用。ソフトで肌あたりの良い着心地です。
オーガニックニ重ガーゼ
パジャマ MEN'S PAJAMAS
紳士・グレー・長袖

表面に凹凸感とシャリ感のある楊柳生地を使用。製品洗いをすることで着慣れた風合いに仕上げました。
綿楊柳チェック
半袖パジャマ LADIES' PAJAMAS
婦人・サックス **M**
バスト79~87

細くしなやかな綿糸を使用した柔らかな肌触りのパジャマです。保湿性、発水性にすぐれ、低刺激の繊維を選びました。
綿ブロード・ウインドチェック
パジャマ MEN'S PAJAMAS
紳士・紺・長袖 **S**
胸囲80~88 身長155~165

有機JASの認定を受けた茶園で栽培した静岡県産の春摘み一番茶です。さわやかな香りと香味が特徴です。
有機日本茶ティーバッグ
煎茶 ORGANIC GREEN TEA BAG
20g(2g×10袋)
336円 無印良品

ポリウレタン入りの糸とナイロン糸を組み合わせて、適度なサポート力を出しました。透明感のよいさくらりとした肌触りです。
ソフトサポートタイプストッキング
ひざ下丈4足組(制電加工) STOCKING
婦人・ナチュラルベージュ・23~25cm
(この商品は23~25cmのものです)
無印良品

左右共通
ジンバブエ綿ガーゼ裏毛パーカー オフ白・グレー・カーキ・紺 S,M,L,LL 税込3,045円(本体価格2,900円)
左ページ
綿ソフトフライスヨーク使いヘンリーネックシャツ オフ白・グレー・カーキ・黒 S,M,L 税込2,625円(本体価格2,500円)
テンセルツイル五分丈パンツ ライトカーキ・カーキ・黒 W58、W61,W64,W67 税込4,095円(本体価格3,900円) 3月上旬発売予定
リボンバレエシューズ 黒 22.5cm~25.0cm 税込3,675円(本体価格3,500円)

Design in Moderation

The essence of fashion is drama, the excitement of happenings and incidents. Fashion throbs with breathtaking energy, the shock of the new burning a hole into convention, or of a cutting-edge object breaking up the aesthetics of the everyday. MUJI does not feed upon this kind of eventfulness. Our aim is to restrain emotion and carefully weave the fruits of human intelligence into products that could be found anywhere: products of exceeding normality that do not belong on either end of any scale.

In copywriters, we look for the ability to "kill poetry." They can't express MUJI poetically. They can't over-utilize words that stir up people's emotions. Text appropriate to MUJI does nothing but give a clear and neutral account of the facts.

We look for the same quality in photographers. They can't make images that rouse people's desires. We want them to take photographs that flawlessly express the answer to the question, "What are we looking at?" By rejecting verbosity, we project a clear vision of the MUJI concept, and the photographs attain their own originality.

Whether designing a package, composing a catalogue, or working on a TV commercial, it's important to keep our distance from trends and carefully avoid

左右共通
インド綿ティアードスカート 白・紺・黒 W58、W61、W64、W67 税込4,725円（本体価格4,500円）3月上旬発売予定
ピンタックボーダーハンドメイドストール オフ白・グレー・ネイビー 37×180cm 税込3,045円（本体価格2,900円）3月中旬発売予定
左ページ
フレンチリネンミドルゲージカーディガン ベージュ・茶 S、M、L、LL 税込4,095円（本体価格3,900円）3月上旬発売予定
インド綿パッチワークスタンドカラーブラウス 白・ライトベージュ・ライトグリーン・黒 S、M、L 税込3,675円（本体価格3,500円）3月中旬発売予定
綿ソフト天竺ラウンドネックシャツ オフ白・ライトパープル・カーキ・黒 S、M、L 税込2,625円（本体価格2,500円）3月中旬発売予定
一枚仕立てクロスストラップ キャメル・黒 S、M、L 税込3,045円（本体価格2,900円）3月上旬発売予定

MUJI catalog, 2006.
————————
Seasonal clothing catalog placed in stores.

reflecting them. Trends in fashion, tones of photographs, types of models and typographic styles change continuously with the flow of time. MUJI does not associate with this ongoing temperamental change. Maintaining a certain style doesn't automatically result in moderate design. But we cannot let our design become simply boring, barren, and cold from trying too hard to distance ourselves from trends.

The important thing is to aspire to design that naturally focuses consciousness on the subject in which MUJI is engaged. If we think of eras progressing in whole numbers, say from 8 to 9 then from 9 to 10 and so on, society will fix its gaze somewhere around 11. But the future may not be found at that point. In fact, the real future is hidden in the small crevices overlooked by society: maybe at 6.8 or 7.3. Just as the discovery of infinite decimal points buried between integers led to a revolution in the level of mathematics, a new awareness of the horizon where objects meet humans will manifest themselves in our ordinary daily lives.

To some people, MUJI may seem to be the last runner on the track. But we are at the forefront, and the art direction for MUJI must reflect that.

Identity and Communication of MUJI | Kenya HARA

無印良品

Magazine ad, 2002.

美しくしたら、目立たなくなりました。

寄せては返す波のように風にもリズムがあります。
時にその不規則なリズムは
人間に心地よさを与えてくれます。
そんな心が自然と落ち着くリズムを
取り入れた扇風機です。
最大の特長は主張しない存在であること。
余計な曲線をなるべくなくし、
地面と平行な台座にすっと伸びた首をつけ、
モーターを覆うパーツも真っすぐな筒にしました。
出しっ放しにしても気にならない
背景に溶け込む美しい扇風機です。

やさしくしよう
無印良品

煙突のある加湿器。

たとえば今は、右斜め前方へ。
潜水艦から顔を出す望遠鏡のようなその煙突で
加湿する方向をコントロールできるため、
壁や棚に蒸気があたり結露する心配がありません。
給水という何気ない行為も毎日繰り返すことを考え、
引き抜く、差し込む、という簡潔な動作だけで
タンクを出し入れできるように。
考え抜いた機能とさりげなく美しい見た目とが
お互いに損なうことなく密やかに同居した、
無印良品の新しい加湿器です。

やさしくしよう
無印良品

Identity and Communication of MUJI | Kenya HARA

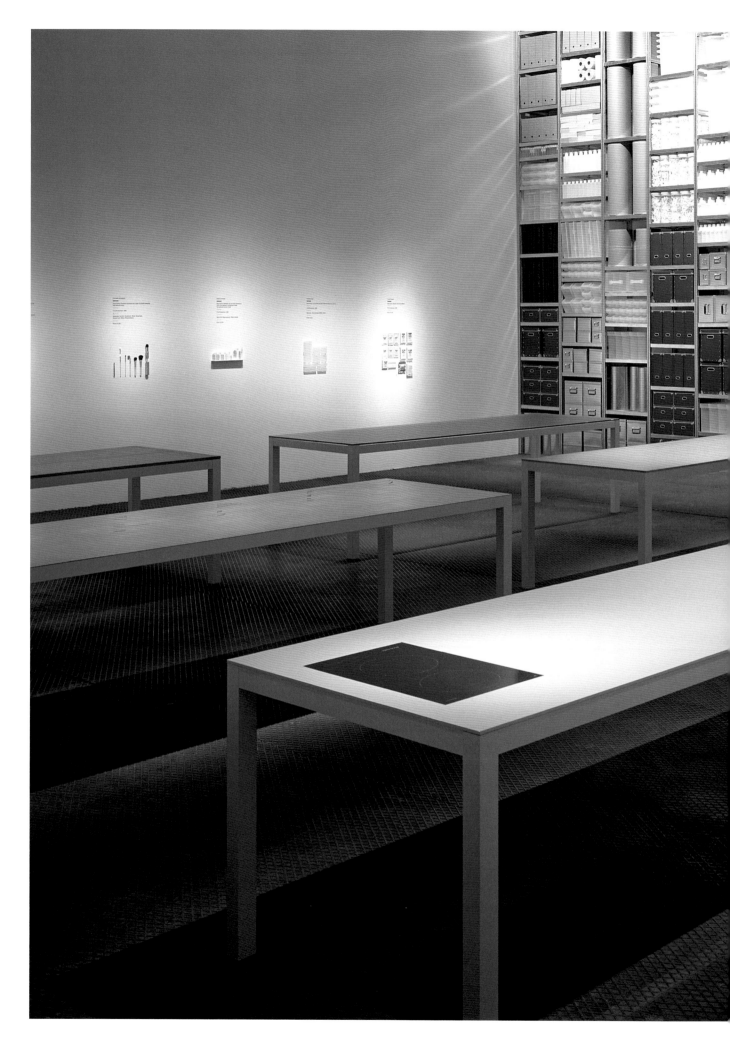

Identity and Communication of MUJI | Kenya HARA

MUJI products stacked to the ceiling,
Milano Salone, 2003.

pp 162-167
Exhibition view, Milano Salone, 2003.

Actual products were displayed on the walls
along with their accompanying text.

At the time, there were no MUJI stores in Italy,
but the exhibition still drew in many
local visitors. The following year,
the first MUJI store opened in Milan.

Identity and Communication of MUJI | Kenya HARA

5 MUJI Space

Takashi SUGIMOTO | Interior Designer

Doing Natural Things Naturally

MUJI opened its first store in 1983, so this year marks its 28th anniversary. Looking at some photos of the first MUJI store, which I hadn't seen in a while, I began to reflect on those early days.

The first MUJI store still exists today, but is quite different now than when it opened. In addition to changes in the products, the interior has also undergone major alterations. I remember well how I had to pull all-nighters because we had so little time before the launch. When I consider how all the ideas that I came up with back then became the framework for all future MUJI stores, I realize that I must have possessed a kind of unconscious intuition or perhaps an image of what MUJI should be: an ideal. For instance, I decided at the time to use worn materials, like aged wood, bricks from demolished buildings, and recycled metal plates for the décor. When I see these materials, which were used in well over 300 MUJI stores, and are still used in some existing ones, I can't help but think, "*This* is MUJI."

When the first MUJI store opened, during the beginning of the bubble era, there was a certain social mood, and retailers competed to build new, beautiful stores. Somewhere within me was a sort of rebellious spirit against this trend, one that was interested in spicing up our daily lives. Looking back, I think it was this spirit that led to such creativity. All MUJI products and spaces are based on the idea of doing natural things naturally, which is perfectly logical, but, in my opinion, something more is needed: a small drop of bitterness, or perhaps even venom. The real essence of creativity, I think, has a little bit of a sting to it.

As MUJI stores developed, various items joined the product line. The types of products were still limited, so we felt like pioneers groping our way through an unknown place as we designed each item to give it a strong sense of purpose in the territory known as MUJI. Stores were opening one after another in Osaka, Kichijoji , Aoyama Sanchome, Sapporo, Yokohama, Fukuoka, Fuchuu, and Hong Kong. The buildings were basically the same overall, but the product line was continuously expanding, so the furnishings and fixtures and the way the products were displayed changed a lot.

The most important thing in the space design process was to maintain a consistent MUJI identity throughout while differentiating MUJI from, and holding our own against, the many designer fashion boutiques opening all over Japan. MUJI

MUJI Space | Takashi SUGIMOTO

pp 171-173
MUJI Aoyama 3-chome, Tokyo, 1993.

This powerful space is constructed
with repurposed pillars and beams
from residential buildings,
and demonstrates the power
of using wood as a structural material.

should be a stylish store, but it shouldn't take a scene from some idealized lifestyle and polish it up until it looks like a scene from a movie. Our intention was to take an extremely ordinary portion of life, to which anyone could relate, and create a space with a little bit of tension—a place where one senses the fundamentals.

As the era progressed and changed gradually but completely, MUJI and the scale of its stores were also transformed. Sales had grown over 100 percent. Some of the earlier stores expanded from 100 to 300 and then to 1000 square meters to accommodate the growing number of products, while some of the new stores were built at 1500 square meters. This period can be called MUJI's "second stage." The head office, which had been part of Seiyu Corporation, achieved independence, and the staff of MUJI, now a company, began to function as a systematic organization. So it was only logical for stores to be planned in detail and built accordingly, with the budget calculated and administered term by term. But because we had never imagined doing things this way, we frequently ran into difficult problems. For one thing, what had been a rough approximation of furnishings and fixtures in the earlier stores became standardized in a manual, and the floors, walls and lighting were nearly standardized as well. As a result, the most important aspect of the store designs became the layout of furnishings and fixtures. It's true that this kind of system allowed us to estimate product volume and production costs with extreme efficiency, but what was really happening to MUJI was an inevitable standardization on all levels.

People in every field have faced this same problem, yet no one has found an effective way to overcome it; I think we are still grappling with it. In any case, time marched on, and after the economic bubble burst, people's lifestyles changed drastically. Designer brands changed, but no one noticed, and sports cars and touring sedans were replaced by so-called "one-box" utilitarian vans. Overall, multipurpose types became the norm. Hotels and inns that once sustained their destinations evolved, and it seems that most of those establishments that haven't been able to adjust to change will go under. The same goes for department stores and large-scale shopping centers. The tumbling economy alone is not responsible for these changes. We, the consumers, are no longer satisfied by the features these businesses offer. Affluence is not about expanding one's desires and buying high performance cars or expensive clothing. No, the most important theme for us now comes in the form of a question: "What should we be seeking in this life?"

MUJI, needless to say, grew into its name over the years. I can still remember clearly when the late Ikko Tanaka first conceived the name. He had posted several possible choices on his office wall, and when we decided on the most overpowering and concise name, the one we felt represented the concept itself, an awkward feeling of embarrassment arose among us. The power and the straightforwardness of the name made us a little nervous; we were overwhelmed. Adding to the impact of the name was its graphic image 無印良品 (*Mujirushi Ryohin*) in large type.

It had such a powerful and direct appeal that it was certain to grab viewers' attention and take them by surprise. Now I realize that it was MUJI's early stage when the initial concepts were being formed that would provide substantial support for MUJI in later years, although MUJI was still a small-scale operation and perhaps didn't have the strongest impact on the public.

There is no question that contradictions abound in what's happening around the world today. This is all the more reason why we must continue in our efforts to emphasize and clearly convey the most important parts of life. I realize that this has become typical in Japan in the 20th century, especially the latter half of the postwar period. In all of the fields in which Japan has manufactured, sold, and won economic power—electric appliances, medicines, clothing, cars, publishing, housing and audio/visual technologies—the contradictions have not been resolved. Yes, there is change and progress, but in reality, the problem is spreading: we have not found satisfaction in our lives; it is actually drifting farther away.

By establishing a strong, concise concept at the start, MUJI was destined to overcome every small contradiction. It became impossible to settle for ordinary products. Even if, as a business, it has a powerful concept at its core, the products must continue to evolve. The stores also cannot peak at a certain level of innovation and just stop. The products must continually make progress, and the stores must constantly communicate this progress. The name of the store is itself a grand creation. This is what fundamentally differentiates MUJI from other businesses. Society is still going through profound changes. We can't see what's ahead, but we do know that this is not a gradual change, like climbing a gentle slope. It's more like climbing a staircase, with each passing step revealing another wall of stairs.

A shop can be seen as a point of sale in which furnishings and fixtures are arrayed. The number of products depends on the number of furnishings and fixtures, while their size and position determine the cost of the store. We might also be able to estimate sales volume from these details. But if we think that way, we can't move forward, nor effectively communicate our concept to the public. As I've said before, MUJI must prevail over every era's contradictions. The greatest of these is the leveling of everything, including products. For customers, a MUJI store must be a source of stimulation that lingers in the most ordinary part of their daily lives. The products are directed to the essential, but avoid eccentricity. It is because of this lack of eccentricity that the stores are given such an important role in communicating the brand's ideals, and therefore must be positioned in the front row of MUJI's creations.

MUJI Sapporo Factory, 1993.

This store uses untouched, original
brick walls from former factory sites.

MUJI Space | Takashi SUGIMOTO

MUJI Space | Takashi SUGIMOTO

MUJI Space | Takashi SUGIMOTO

MUJI Space | Takashi SUGIMOTO

[リニューアルオープン限定]
白磁

MUJI Space | Takashi SUGIMOTO

pp 176-183
MUJI Yurakucho, 2001.

MUJI's largest store, carrying over 7,500
items. Included in the retail complex are
the café/deli/bakery Café & Meal MUJI,
the flower shop Hana Ryohin,
and a MUJI HOUSE showroom.

pp 184-189
MUJI Tokyo Midtown, Roppongi, Tokyo,
2007.

This is the first international MUJI store
in Japan. It showcases an array of carefully
selected items, including the clothing line
MUJI LABO and the interior design
component Real Furniture.
For furniture purchases, items come in
a variety of sizes, and advice
on furniture coordination is also available.

MUJI Tokyo Midtown

I would call this MUJI's "third stage," a period during which the era's contradictions have become apparent to the greater public to some degree. In my opinion, this stage is in effect now in areas of central Tokyo like Roppongi Hills, Tokyo Midtown, and Marunouchi. The basic concepts behind these recently developed urban environments are actually conventional ideologies that have been refined and expanded. Nevertheless, I recognize an undeniable sense of perplexity in the management or in those peoples' occupations that conventional thought cannot penetrate. And many people there are trying to fit in but somehow can't.

MUJI Tokyo Midtown was planned during this era of ambiguity. However, this store was to be a return to the original concept and a contemporary restructuring of MUJI. This was an experiment to organize the materials, reduce the rather excessive customer service, and lessen the consumer's consciousness of the products themselves. The goal was to entrust the store with MUJI's philosophy—to use the space to start again from first principles and reinforce the particular philosophy we'd always been after. It may sound too serious, but life today is of course quite a bit more difficult for all of us, and isn't going to lighten up very easily. We always have to think and worry about everything. This might be another contradiction of our times, but one solution is to eliminate all excess as if chopping it off with a hatchet in order to keep our minds clean and fresh. It's hard to do, but that's why we long for it.

In the past, even just thirty years ago, downtowns flourished: department stores were absolutely stuffed with customers, streets were crowded, pedestrian overflow from some avenues restricted vehicle access. Real estate and the stock market were rising steadily, and our desires were constantly aroused. The future shone brightly.

But that era is gone, and we have climbed to the next stage in the staircase of time. We face a new horizon. Every day we hear concerns about self-sustenance, the safety of the food we eat and energy consumption, and witness strong interest in restricting carbon dioxide emissions. In other words, the glamour to which products used to aspire is a thing of the past.

MUJI started out with products such as "cracked rice crackers," "broken-up and dried shiitake mushrooms" and "fractured udon noodles." The slogan was, "Lower Priced for a Reason." This is where everything began, the point from which MUJI expanded.

Now in its third stage, MUJI should not only build upon its base, but also take a step forward and set aside its value of relativity in order to find another, independent value. Just as people are very attuned to the quality of food, they are

MUJI Space | Takashi SUGIMOTO

looking for a reliability of materials and depth of care in the products they buy; this is one solution for us. We can carefully examine various fabrics used around the world since ancient times, like cotton, wool and linen, and choose the one most suited for the product. Instead of using mass-production equipment, we can use classic weaving machines that allow some help from the human hand, despite the fact that this decreases productivity. In these ways, I believe that MUJI must become something like slow food.

From the steps that we stand on today, high productivity is not a priority. We are reconsidering how we think and what our purpose is. Instead of competing with other stores on daily sales volume, we are looking for ways to distinctly convey a proper image to the customers and make them think about the beauty and the very essence of MUJI.

MUJI does not showcase mass-produced items and compete on production costs. On the contrary, MUJI wants to act as a magnetic field where one can slim down an excessive life, pursue the basic essence of things, and feel and share the resulting beauty for which MUJI strives.

MUJI Space | Takashi SUGIMOTO

MUJI Space | Takashi SUGIMOTO

MUJI Space | Takashi SUGIMOTO

MUJI Space | Takashi SUGIMOTO

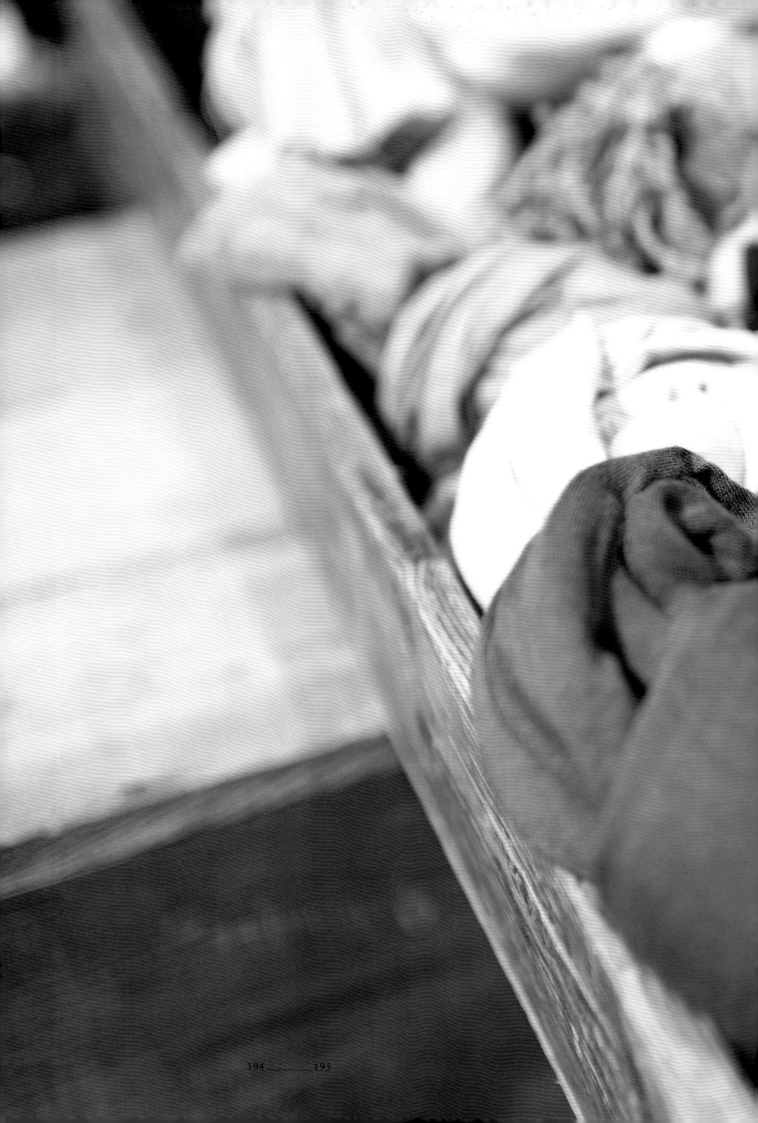

MUJI Space | Takashi SUGIMOTO

MUJI Space | Takashi SUGIMOTO

MUJI Space | Takashi SUGIMOTO

pp 190-203
MUJI Shinjuku, 2008.

Cozier than the Roppongi branch
(MUJI Tokyo Midtown),
MUJI Shinjuku includes
Café & Meal MUJI
and an open display space
for Real Furniture.

pp 204-207
MUJI to GO, Nagoya Chubu Centrair
International Airport, 2009

MUJI to GO focuses on items
that pertain to travel and business,
and is available at select airports and
train stations.

pp 209-217
MUJI Wood House.

In this open studio with an atrium,
the occupant can freely "edit" the living
space. Built according to SE (Safety
Engineering) codes, the structure is
fortified with supporting pillars and beams.

MUJI HOUSE

It has been some time since MUJI HOUSE was first conceived, developed, and sold as a series. Now there are three lines: "Wood House," "Window House" and "Morning House." These don't look like they sprang from the same line of thought, and we can't clearly foresee how each will evolve. This may be due to the difficulty of turning conceptual housing into a business and the complicated structure of the MUJI HOUSE philosophy. Or, perhaps the project's unpredictable course of trial and error means that it is not yet fully developed.

Because MUJI now carries more household goods, consumer electronics, home appliances and furniture, we considered making houses as an extension of our products. However, it's almost impossible to realize the concept "Lower Priced for a Reason" in the housing business. We could use it as a catchphrase, but the systemization of this mature and fiercely competitive field has been developed, maintained and dominated by just a few major companies. And established sales processes are not comparable to those for household goods or clothing.

In my opinion, MUJI HOUSE should not be expensive, for its priority is not cost, nor should it be simply oriented towards aesthetics. It should tower at the border of the strong frontier that is the MUJI lifestyle, where it must contradict other, easily homogenized concepts. Like the idea I emphasized in MUJI Space, it should represent a "natural" territory of special and thoughtful design, emphatic of the everyday life. We want customers not to aim for homogeneity, but to interact with the nature of living without extra things and with objects made of carefully selected materials, while taking a secret pleasure and pride in living in MUJI HOUSE.

The current goal for MUJI HOUSE is not to amplify the existing series but to revise its products by reconsidering the details and materials, increasing the choices, exploring the affluence of moderation in the use of space, and exhibiting the pinnacle of MUJI style in a model of inner space or, in other words, of daily living.

MUJI HOUSE is destined to be a limited residential space. No doubt, one can make a fine living there, but it *is* compact. The proper solution here is not to try to expand the space but to provide storage, bath and kitchen areas rationally designed to fit within a compact area. Most importantly, it should afford plenty of communication. Also crucial is the right selection of building materials. We do not plan to lower the cost by using cheap materials in competition with other companies, but rather, to allow each customer's taste to determine them. We seek a space that's small but full of substance. Imagine something along the lines of a Japanese tearoom in a contemporary style, or a bungalow in a big city, but surrounded by greenery. MUJI HOUSE is a proposition for a living space for people who feel, enjoy, and understand the subtly different aspects of beauty that reside in everyday life.

MUJI Space | Takashi SUGIMOTO

MUJI Space | Takashi SUGIMOTO

MUJI Space | Takashi SUGIMOTO

MUJI Space | Takashi SUGIMOTO

MUJI Space | Takashi SUGIMOTO

pp 218-219
MUJI Window House.

Windows can be placed anywhere in
this house. You can cut a hole out of
any part of its walls to enjoy the scenery
outside like a picture in a frame.

MUJI Space | Takashi SUGIMOTO

Shiroi Komachi Project, 2010.

A city planning project for Shiroi City in Chiba Prefecture, consisting of a neighborhood of MUJI Houses.

MUJI Space | Takashi SUGIMOTO

MUJI Campgrounds

MUJI manages three campgrounds in Japan:
Tsunan in Niigata Prefecture,
Minami Norikura in Gifu Prefecture,
and Campagna Tsumagoi in Gunma Prefecture.
Having eliminated excess services,
MUJI offers a pure place to enjoy nature,
along with outdoor education
and summer camps for kids.

Tsunan Campground, 1995.

Located in Niigata Prefecture's Tsunan
Village. This campground affords a
panoramic view of the adjacent
900-meter Yamabushi Mountain, and below,
the Shinano River that has created
the largest river terrace in Japan.

Minami Norikura Campground, 1996.

Gifu Prefecture alpine meadow.
To the north is Norikura highland,
and to the south, majestic mountains.
Thanks to the elevation of this plateau (1600m),
visitors can experience the precious
natural sub-alpine wildflowers.

Campagna Tsumagoi, 2004.

On the Baragi Plateau in Hoshimata, the village of
Tsumagoi, Agatsuma District, in Gunma Prefecture.
Encircled by Mount Asama, one of the top 100 mountains of Japan;
Shirane Mountain and Azumaya Mountain,
this plateau is 1300m above sea level.
Fishing and canoeing are popular activities here.

pp 224-225
Image from "MUJI Campground" campaign, 2005.
pp 226-227
Image from "MUJI Campground" campaign, 2008.
pp 228-229
Image from "MUJI Campground" campaign, 2009.

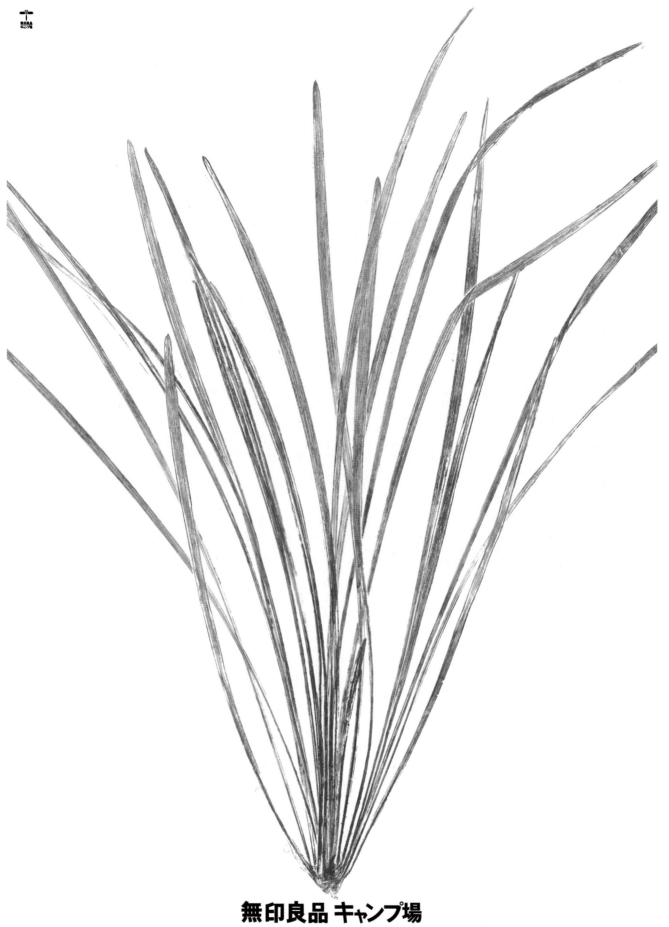

無印良品 キャンプ場
www.mujioutdoor.net

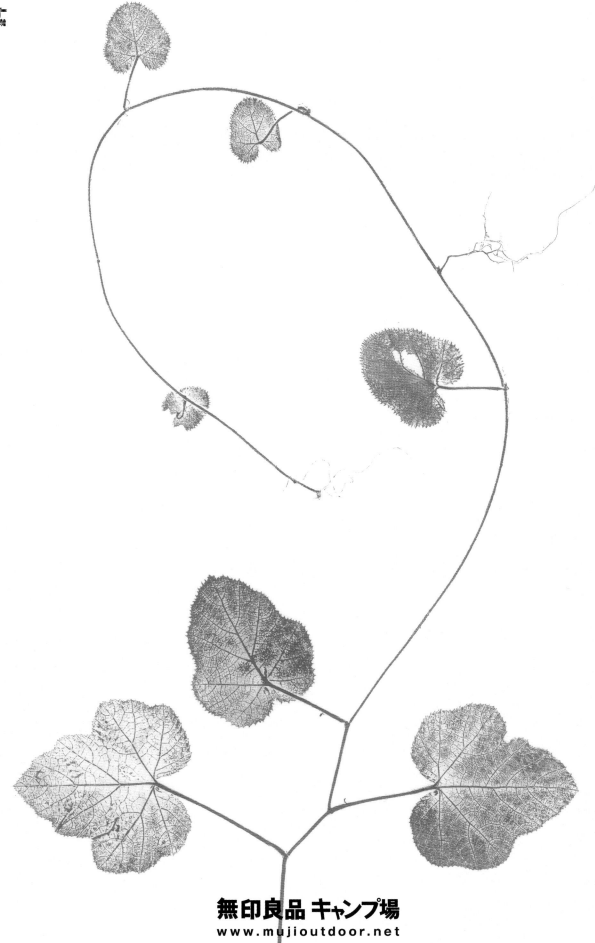

無印良品 キャンプ場
www.mujioutdoor.net

MUJI Space | Takashi SUGIMOTO

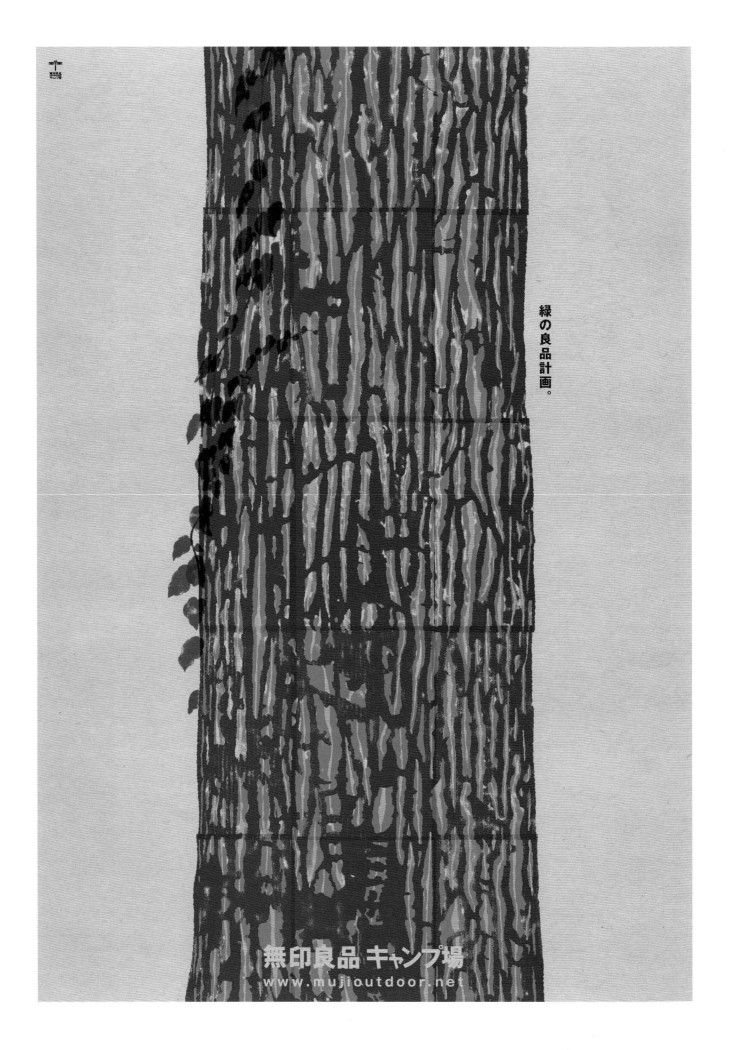

緑の良品計画。

無印良品 キャンプ場
www.mujioutdoor.net

緑の良品計画。

MUJI Space │ Takashi SUGIMOTO

地球にやさしくされましょう。

無印良品 キャンプ場
www.mujioutdoor.net

地球にやさしくされましょう。

無印良品 キャンプ場
www.mujioutdoor.net

MUJI Space │ Takashi SUGIMOTO

Mujirushi Ryohin BGM 1980-2000

A 3-CD set of in-store BGM from 1980,
when MUJI was established as
Seiyu's private brand. At the time,
creating original BGM was an
innovative gesture.

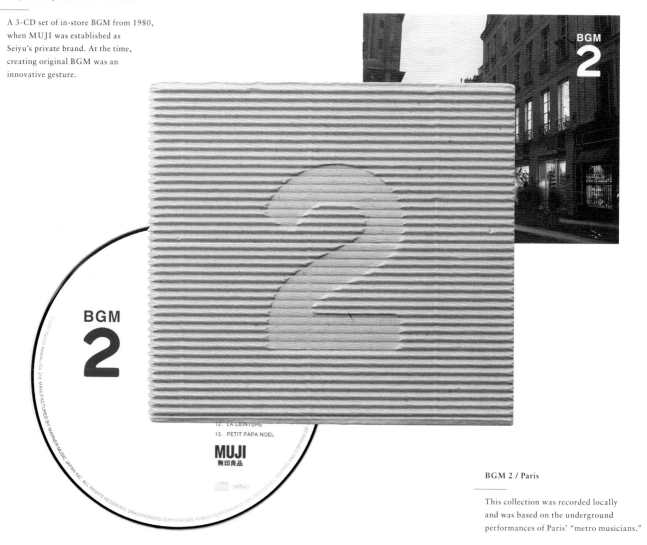

BGM 2 / Paris

This collection was recorded locally
and was based on the underground
performances of Paris' "metro musicians."

MUJI Background Music

Music rooted in the history and cultures of various cities
around the world is performed by local
musicians and recorded by MUJI.
These recordings are played in MUJI stores and also sold as CDs.
Since 2000, MUJI has produced 17 CDs.

BGM 3 / Sicily

An anthology of traditional music played
by local musicians of the Sicilian city
of Taormina, led by pianist Scimone.

BGM 4 / Ireland

This CD of traditional music,
recorded by Dublin musicians,
harkens back to traditional life on Ireland.

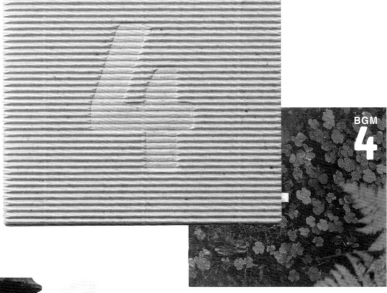

BGM 5 / Puerto Rico

Musicians in San Juan, capital of
the beautiful Caribbean island of
Puerto Rico, recorded music of
the Jivaroan peoples for this CD.

BGM 6 / Andalusia

This CD of traditional music was recorded
locally in Andalusia, land of flamenco
and bullfighting,
by the Roman musician Sevilla.

MUJI Space | Takashi SUGIMOTO

6 The Future of MUJI: A Conversation

Recorded on December 18th, 2009.
The participants were
the five authors of this book.

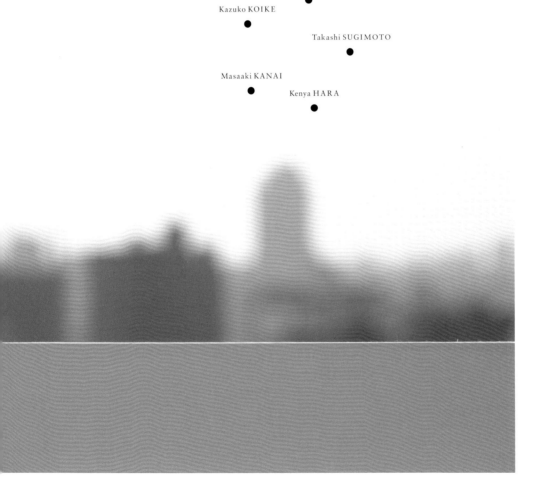

Naoto FUKASAWA

Kazuko KOIKE

Takashi SUGIMOTO

Masaaki KANAI

Kenya HARA

Kenya HARA

Takashi SUGIMOTO

Approaching New Territory

HARA: Today, the five of us have gathered to discuss MUJI, as we often do. The first topic is "new territory," specifically, where and how MUJI will develop and expand. I think it would be interesting for us to start by talking about MUJI HOTEL, which has surfaced in our discussions from time to time.

SUGIMOTO: It's probably been well over ten years since we first started talking about hotels. This is not because we are particularly attracted to the hotel business, but because—in every era since its founding—MUJI has devoted itself to developing products. So there must be something that can programmatically feature this range of goods. We felt that, hypothetically, a hotel could fit the bill. If my memory is correct, it all started when we were contacted by the owner of a *pension*, or Western-style boardinghouse, on Sado Island in the Japan Sea. He was a big fan of MUJI and wanted to use MUJI furniture and fixtures throughout his establishment. MUJI cooperated fully and MUJI fans started visiting the *pension*, sometimes writing us thank-you notes about their marvelous experiences. We realized that a hotel could be an integrated template for the MUJI concept. So now, when I'm developing new products, I ask myself, "Could it be used in a hotel?" Of course, there are things that aren't used in hotels, but the idea is, could the product have a certain significance in a private room or public space of a hotel? Business hotels are gaining popularity. The idea of staying in a hotel to work or experience the relaxation

of a resort is becoming more rooted in people's lifestyles. So at one point we thought, "Why not just make a 'MUJI HOTEL' and see how MUJI furniture, clothing and food look there?" I think we may able to realize this idea sometime soon. In order to increase the number of people who are interested in MUJI we need a new and powerful domain in which to display the MUJI-type lifestyle and MUJI-type activities thoroughly, and it's time we consider this idea seriously. The thirtieth anniversary might be good timing to realize this type of space.

HARA: MUJI is not simply a group of products. It's more like an engine of thought for the purpose of creating products. So in order to talk about what MUJI is, we simply need a fresh, new vehicle in which to place MUJI. A hotel is great for that purpose. Mr. Sugimoto talked about a very functional hotel, but I imagine an advanced resort hotel. More people are working not only in their offices, but also while traveling around the world, so I feel that the cutting-edge resorts in the future will be something like natural surroundings studded with high-tech cottages—a kind of futuristic MUJI resort. How about everyone else? What do you imagine a "MUJI HOTEL" to be?

KOIKE: As a prototype, I also imagine a city hotel with a nice ambiance like Mr. Sugimoto described: one in which people have a clear image of MUJI. In cities like Kyoto, for example, there are remarkably simple business hotels that specialize in "stay-only" plans. They remain cost conscious by not serving breakfast, and this also helps customers

Masaaki KANAI

experience the local culture by going out to break-fast somewhere in the Nishiki Market. But, the customer has to endure some disadvantages as far as the comfort level goes. I expect MUJI HOTEL to be a place that reveals the wisdom and details of living that MUJI has accumulated. One of the great purposes of the hotel is to make these details and this wisdom tangible so that people who have not noticed them yet will pay attention.

FUKASAWA: Well, I also feel that the idea is interesting, of making a hotel the size of a business hotel as a compilation of MUJI's ideas on living and producing a balanced comfort, not doing it as a form of business. However, I do think it's better to avoid the image of a real business hotel, which would be exactly what you'd feel if we simply placed a small modular tub and basic MUJI toiletry set in every room and a sauna on the top floor that you can enter with a special coupon. No, instead, I'd like to see something like a condensed view of high-quality living, like a testing ground for an environment where, for example, neat pillows and clean MUJI sheets are always supplied. If we did it that way, I can imagine a real MUJI HOTEL existing.

KOIKE: Indeed.

FUKASAWA: In order to achieve an ideal level of quality, the hotel needs cleanliness, warmth, and good service. Just fixing it up with simple, MUJI-like interior design would produce a somewhat weakened effect. We have to make sure we construct it in such a way that the MUJI ideology is conveyed with aplomb.

SUGIMOTO: So, what you're talking about is a hotel that clarifies the MUJI concept, not just a hotel full of MUJI products, right? I think that people use MUJI products not only because of the lower prices, but because using them gives one a feeling of relief, or maybe brings a little smile. I want to take that feeling, you know, and incorporate it into people's outlook on life. MUJI HOUSE is still somewhat ambiguous. It has the clear mandate of making people feel that, "Living in this house will really enrich our hearts," but it falls a step short because of various barriers, legal and otherwise. I believe MUJI HOTEL is the next step beyond MUJI HOUSE. Of course, it'll be far more economical than today's three- and four-star hotels, but I don't want to call it a business hotel. I'm imagining a place where people stay during some break in their schedules and emerge thinking, "That was nice," or, "Today was a good day." I think they could even be in resort areas. I bet they'd be a hit in places like Atami or Kanagawa (laughs). The common Japanese resort hotel today, with its exaggerated dinners with countless small dishes, and open-air baths in every room—constantly running, even if the guests only use them twice a day—is an expression of maximum extravagance and anything but environmentally conscious. This brings up a strong desire for a category of hotels that are reasonably priced and yet satisfying to our souls.

KANAI: Once, I stayed at a *ryokan* [a traditional Japanese inn] in Izu, Kanagawa, in a room with

Naoto FUKASAWA

no extra objects and only a *futon* with pure white cotton sheets and duvet covers. That night, I slept extremely well, so the next morning, I asked the hotel staff what kind of *futon* it was. The reply was, "We just let it air in the sun everyday." Both the sheets and duvet cover were made of good materials that were simply clean and white. I said to myself, "Ahh! *This* is MUJI!" Then I began to notice that most of the articles they used at the inn—slippers, wastebaskets, towels, toothbrushes, and cups—actually *were* MUJI. That must have been a "MUJI HOTEL."

HARA: I think it would be quite interesting if a MUJI HOTEL were built in a city with great futuristic potential, like Berlin, and run with the kind of Japanese hospitality described by Mr. Kanai. In Japan, we have the *ryokan* system of lodging, which is rarely seen anywhere else in the world. Even within Asia, I think there aren't many other countries with a native accommodation service that can compete at the level of the Western five-stars; no matter what *other* country or region you visit, the highest ranked hotel is usually Western-style. The way a *ryokan* proprietress cares for her guests and presents ikebana (arranged flowers) is a welcome of the highest standards, and I'm thinking of ways to incorporate that into a hotel operation. In a MUJI HOTEL, everything—furnishings, fixtures and the service that lies behind them—must be equally supremely simple and of high quality.

Creating the Future for Housing and Living

FUKASAWA: I'm always thinking about "more comfortable living," proposing ways of living through design, and doing my best to convey them in an easily understandable manner. But lately I've been brooding over the fact that no matter how hard I try, there doesn't seem to be any change in the way people live their lives. As someone who makes things, I would think that this was my fault. In desperation, I would say, "How about if I try this, or that?" Now I'm starting to realize that it's not because of me, but because most people aren't making tasteful use of designed products in their lives, or rather because no one is teaching them how. There are many who think that by simply buying good products, their lifestyles will automatically improve, but without thinking about how they might reasonably capitalize on and use these objects in their lifestyles, in the end, their houses will remain cluttered. MUJI provides many products that can enhance lives, but the fact is, lifestyles don't change so easily. I feel that this sensibility surrounding one's lifestyle is entirely lacking today.

SUGIMOTO: Until around the Meiji period, that sensibility was a part of regular households, as was some sense of tension.

FUKASAWA: That's right.

HARA: Over the past 50 years in Japan, our life-

Kazuko KOIKE

styles, our families, our communities and our working lives have undergone a drastic transformation. So no one can teach us what I would call, "a wise way to live." Fathers can't teach it to their children, and schools can't teach it to their students. So we need to plow everything under, as one would plow a field. This is a restructuring of desire—about what kind of house we want to live in and what kinds of things we want to surround us. If we can establish in society something like, "home and living expertise," I think that even in Japan a comfortable, sustainable lifestyle will emerge. Now that MUJI carries between 5,000 and 7,000 products, we're not going to be able to see the future of MUJI unless we continue thinking about and working on that issue.

KOIKE: What we inherited from the previous generation is a certain way of living, and lately I've begun to believe that if we don't make efforts to re-inherit it, we're out of luck. So wouldn't it be great if something like this MUJI HOTEL that we've been talking about could act as a place of education about ways of living, where users, or clients, would naturally comprehend this inheritance? Considering the current condition of Japan, I feel a sense of crisis when it comes to, "lifestyle education," or, "the aesthetics of living."

FUKASAWA: "The aesthetics of living." That's a nice phrase.

KOIKE: Ikko Tanaka was fond of the aesthetics of living, wasn't he?

HARA: I feel a seedling of that growing in The Laboratory of Superior Items for Living that Ms. Koike started on the web. By soliciting opinions through the Internet, we can see that there's really a remarkably strong interest among people for living well, and not in the sense of living richly, but simply living with good sense.

KOIKE: Yes, and because we group the requests by action, not by product, like, "How do you clean your house?" we get countless posts, like, "I've always said that a feather duster and a rag are the best," or, "A broom is good." It was truly eye-opening for me to learn that behind the quiet and reserved voice of the Japanese people was such a strong desire for living better, meaning more reasonably, effectively and comfortably.

FUKASAWA: That kind of living takes a lot of time and effort, but expending time and effort for better living leads to peace, right?

KOIKE: I agree. And, we've only just started working on this. I'm realizing that this is just building the foundation for giving proper thought to our lives and living spaces.

SUGIMOTO: But what about the people who shoulder the burden of the household? Don't you think they would be reluctant to expend the time and effort necessary to think about these kinds of things? It's not only in Japan, but everywhere in today's world seems quite difficult to restore that ideology.

Kazuko KOIKE

HARA: Well, whether or not we can go back to our traditions, to the Japanese, cleaning is the ultimate expression of the meaningful tradition known as *shitsurai*. *Shitsurai* is not just the decoration of a room with seasonal objects and colors symbolic of a special occasion, like New Year's Day, but is a very important aesthetic element of hospitality. A Zen temple is clean not only because of the orderly nature of the *shoji* latticework and frame or the balance of the dry landscape garden known as *karesansui*, but actually because someone is constantly cleaning the temple as part of the ascetic practice of Zen Buddhism. Nature, left alone, falls to ruin. So someone has to pull the weeds and rake the fallen leaves. But too much of that cleanliness makes it artificial, so on the temple grounds, rocks are left covered with moss and some fallen leaves remain. That's how a Zen temple keeps itself at what we call the, "shoreline," or the boundary, between nature and artificiality. It's difficult, but the concept doesn't ever get old.

FUKASAWA: Recently I reread Soetsu Yanagi's writing about *mingei*, or folkcrafts, and I realized that since the beauty of *mingei* is an aesthetics rooted in the lifestyles of ordinary people, it corresponds with what MUJI is doing; I thought, you know, that this is the design that we're doing. During the period of *mingei*'s popularity, people honored and respected harmony and did not boast to one another of being richer than others. Instead they felt that living more simply or doing well with fewer resources were superior abilities that demonstrated a high level of lifestyle aesthetics. Today, we don't talk about lifestyle aesthetics. Back in

those days, I think people were trained in home discipline, like, "Fold a rag neatly and then hang it up," or, "Pull out the corners of a pillow to make it square." Today people consider these niceties troublesome, but back when they were practiced, I'll bet food was simple but delicious.

KANAI: The theme of a "better life" has always been discussed in the world of design, and even ages ago, before the word "design" existed, humankind consistently pursued a "better life" by working and creating objects. As a result, human life has become full of objects, or perhaps flooded with them. Ms. Koike has used the phrase, "A lifestyle that feels good." When MUJI first came into existence, our motto was, "Clothes that feel good to wear, food that's good to eat, and objects that are useful in life," and our goal was to provide reasonably priced products to satisfy humankind's basic needs. Now, we must add to that self-control and concern for the earth our manufacturers, and other people, all of which will become connected to this, "lifestyle that feels good." Through projects like The Laboratory of Superior Items for Living, MUJI can perform research and hold discussions from the same point of view as ordinary people living their lives, and I think it's going to get more interesting as we go on.

KOIKE: Because the processes of cleaning and washing ultimately connect to environmental issues and ecology, through repeated discussions, we can begin to rework the social structure within, from which products are generated. For example, if we state that it's better to clean naturally

The Future of MUJI: A Conversation

Naoto FUKASAWA

using baking soda, we become the antithesis to the chemical detergent industry, and it would be great if we could develop a network with companies and NPOs that share these ideas. The Laboratory of Superior Items for Living questions ordinary people and is also starting to exchange opinions with specialists who make detergents. Looking at this optimistically, it seems we have a chance to implement positive ecology.

HARA: I think that "a lifestyle that feels good" comes from those kinds of efforts. When people hear words like, "cool" or "stylish", or "better," they can't help but become competitive or aggressive. When we're dealing with a lifestyle, we should think first about how we can create one that pleases our neighbors, before we begin to consider ecology or whatever else. For example, when you're building a house, you don't want your neighbors to think, jealously, "I hate that big mansion next door!" They will accept you much more if their response is instead, "Thanks to that well-balanced house, my house looks better too." This way of living is more advanced, of higher quality and smarter than flaunting one's wealth, though it is quite difficult to pull off.

FUKASAWA: When something "feels good" or "has a good atmosphere," the individuality and form of the thing has disappeared. When there is complete unity, the individuality of each thing disappears, so the only expressions you can come up with to describe the situation are, "It's really nice," or, "This feels good." These indicate a high level of perfection. But if you try to achieve the

same effect through a particular object, then the object stands out too much, and the only feedback you will hear is, "This place is nice because of this nice object." The balance has collapsed. Using the metaphor of ground and figure, to make food on a table look good, the plate is the background, or ground; to make the plate look beautiful, the table becomes the ground. The relationship between ground and figure is in constant flux. But if you keep in mind the balance between the ground and the figure, you get a situation where the whole entity is good. Up until now, the majority of design has been about making the figure. I feel that design and the making of things are going in the wrong direction. There is this desperate effort to create the thing, the figure, and then when all the elements are gathered together, the whole is a chaotic mess. But because objects are going to exist whether we like it or not, MUJI performs an erasure, of sorts, of their individuality. MUJI does not allow objects to assert themselves; we use transparent or unbleached materials so that the object can become the background. Still, this is just a physical strategy. I feel that MUJI is now at the next stage, in which we can test this concept of whether things can be literally removed, and whether forms can be erased. Of course, we need to sell our products, so it's absolutely crucial that we appeal to the sensibilities of potential customers. We have truly entered the next stage.

World MUJI

HARA: I have been using the phrase "education of desire" to describe the cultivation of desire for

Kenya HARA

Masaaki KANAI

living in the Japanese market, but I know it's going to be a long and tedious process that will show results five or even ten years from now. On the other hand, widening our viewpoint to include the entire globe, we see particularly huge markets like China and India, and there's no question that Asia will become the center of the world's consumerism. When I realize that international sales will eventually surpass domestic volume for MUJI, I get the feeling that taking lots of hints from China, for instance, would be a good way to take advantage of an opportunity to begin thinking about new things. If, as Mr. Fukasawa has said, the "world of moderation" is an extremely powerful precedent for Japan, what about when we expand into the Chinese market? Can we take that same thinking with us? Will it be convincing to the people there? What do you all think?

FUKASAWA: I think that in China, the very basic lifestyle that is MUJI's foundation still exists in reality. Compared to Japan, where most cities were so chaotically modernized, China retains great charm that remains, as yet, untouched. But China is still in the throes of insatiable materialism, if we can call it that, making and consuming things with incredible speed and vigor, and thus undergoing exaggerated growth and complexity, so I don't expect it to begin eliminating things to the point where only the good feeling remains, as we have started doing in Japan. However, that's all the more reason for MUJI to continue to give suggestions and seek further expansion in China.

HARA: What about the concept of cleaning and

sustainability that we were talking about before? We share the same basic sense of what this "aesthetics of living" is, which is why MUJI is successful in the domestic market. But will it work in China? If MUJI should propose refinement merely as a style, there's a possibility that people will lose interest the moment they understand the concept.

KOIKE: Well, I think it's about the creation of desire. The desire to keep things in a particular order can't be forced by someone else, so all MUJI can do is to provide the products and the space, and hope that people will recognize the good feeling they engender.

HARA: The goal is for people to have a dramatic experience of "feeling good" and awaken to the fact that a space can be made beautiful not by adding something new but by just eliminating the clutter that surrounds modern living.

FUKASAWA: I think that would be difficult to manage. It's like eating ramen in a tidy new restaurant; it doesn't taste very good, because there's this culture of the old, somewhat grimy ramen shop, right? Maybe if we start at the aesthetic apex in each country, it would work. Here in Japan, Katsura Imperial Villa and Ise Grand Shrine represent the aesthetic apex, and reflect values wedded to a particular place, and fundamentally they are venues for purification. A similar site in Mainland China would reflect the same sublime purity, and would be a perfect model.

KOIKE: Accepted aesthetics differ from country

Takashi SUGIMOTO

to country and aesthetics is a very subtle issue. The sense of what's pure and orderly depends on the country and the land.

KANAI: Going back to the ramen shops, sometimes here in Japan there will be an old ramen shop that's got a lot of character, and even though it's popular the way it is, they'll renovate it into a nice, clean place, and with that one fell swoop, the charm drops by half!

HARA: Japan may be a little abnormal in this hypersensitivity, in fact. Whenever I return to Japan from abroad, it's astounding that to my mind, the cleanliness of the airport overshadows the unsophisticated architecture. I feel that I could lie down on the shining tiles, and even though there are some spots on the carpet, there's evidence that someone has at least tried to remove them. Our roads are smooth, and our public streetlights are never flickering, or burned out. Japanese culture expects every person to carry a certain responsibility of his or her own, whether building something or preparing food. I don't know if we should call it aesthetics or common sense, but I know it's a resource our country has. MUJI should think of it as a resource and make use of it.

KANAI: From that point of view, we think of MUJI as being universal. When we establish new stores and operate outside of Japan, we don't think it's wise to bring our Japanese staff members, with their excellent knowledge of MUJI, and make them the core of the operation. We prefer the local staff take on as much of the operation as they can,

because they often give us ideas that we'd never come up with on our own. In the future, the overseas market will definitely grow to be larger than the domestic market, so it's important that we don't simply bring over everything designed and created in Japan by Japanese people, but rather, we create MUJI together with the local people. Generally speaking, Western brands don't do this kind of thing. Instead, they mostly choose to maintain a firm hold on the brand by giving someone from the original location all the basic controls. But MUJI must work differently and develop from our characteristic of turning the concept into products. I don't think MUJI can grow otherwise.

KOIKE: I'm very interested in this network of designers that Mr. Hara has started in China.

HARA: Well, whether we're conveying the culture of cleaning or whatever else, the core part of the concept can't be left out. For this we need a creative director, but it's also necessary to appoint talented local designers. In every part of the world into which we advance, it's about how much we can draw out the unique elements of the location and enjoy what we do while also protecting the concept's core. If it's China, then it's very important to consider what kind of soul we put into the concept behind the four-character word 無印良品 as it will exist in China. MUJI's vision is to imagine, "If MUJI had been created first in China, what would MUJI have become?" We're not attempting to infuse the rest of the world with the universality of Japanese culture. What we want to do is to create a structure by which MUJI can absorb into its core the advantages of all the cultures, attach ideas to each region that are really going to be absorbed and stick, and produce a new concept from all that. This doesn't mean, however, that MUJI can be interpreted and expanded without limits right from the beginning, or else everything will collapse. (laughs) It's going to be difficult but important to maintain the life of the concept, while maintaining control. If this were a game of tennis we would just give a racket to the local designers and serve the ball, hoping that they will hit it back to us with a Chinese interpretation of MUJI.

KOIKE: Decades ago, Ikko Tanaka and I had a conversation about how China is "full of 'MUJI'", meaning full of MUJI-like things, and we suppressed a wry smile. I guess that when we sense that the vigor of things has remained unchanged for so long, we can't help but expect it to symbolize something.

HARA: We can say China is "full of 'MUJI'" because those words were spoken by the late Ikko Tanaka, whose eyes were as sharp as those of the 16th century tea master, Sen no Rikyu, but the Chinese don't see it that way at all.

KOIKE: That's the point. And the same is true in Japan, too. There are things in our lives that are so ordinary we notice them only when foreign brands tell us, "This is what we like about Japan." That kind of mutual influence is absolutely necessary.

KANAI: I think so, too. There are many cases in which someone from overseas discovered some miscellaneous thing that we Japanese had been taking for granted, and only then did we notice its value.

SUGIMOTO: That's a good thing. There may not be value to every single thing, but if there's value to discover, MUJI will find it, right? It's like a slowly but steadily flowing river; we can't expect to see the same scenery forever.

List of Sources
and Credits

Remarkable Umbrella
2006
p 017
Product designer: Konstantin Grcic

Pine 5-Shelf Wide Unit
2008
p 027

Image from the "Like Water" Campaign
2009
pp 004-011
Location: New York, Istanbul, Beijing, Rome
Art director: Kenya Hara
Photographer: Yoshihiko Ueda

left to right:
**Cutlery—Table Fork, Dessert Fork,
Table Knives, Dessert Knives, Butter Spreader,
Table Spoon, Dessert Spoon, Tea Spoon,
Soup Spoon, Long Spoon**
2007
pp 020-021
Product designer: Jasper Morrison

Recycled Kraft Paper Notebook
2009
p 023

"Lower Priced for a Reason."
newspaper ad | 1980
p 029
Size: B1
Creative director: Ikko Tanaka
Art director: Hiroshi Kojitani
Copy writer: Kazuko Koike
Illustrator: Shigeo Fukuda

"Love Doesn't Beautify."
newspaper ad | 1981
p 031
Size: B1
Creative director: Ikko Tanaka
Art director: Hiroshi Kojitani
Graphic designer: Kensuke Irie
Copywriter: Kazuko Koike
Illustrator: Yuzo Yamashita

**Men's 90-Degree Angle Stripe Socks,
Charcoal gray**
2006
p 015
Photographer: Asuka Katagiri
*For all pages onward until p027

Recycled Kraft Paper Notebook Diary
2008
p 025

"The whole salmon is salmon."
newspaper ad | 1981
p 033
Size: B1
Creative director: Ikko Tanaka
Art director: Hiroshi Kojitani
Copywriter: Kazuko Koike
Illustrator: Yuzo Yamashita

MUJI Store, Aoyama, Tokyo
1983 | p 035, pp 036-037
Interior designer: Takashi Sugimoto
Photographer: Yoshio Shiratori, pp 036-037

"A Stack of Moments: Life"
poster | 1993
p 041
Size: B1
Creative director: Ikko Tanaka, Kazuko Koike
Art director: Masaaki Hiromura
Photographer: Takashi Oyama
Graphic designer: Toshiyuki Kojima
Copywriter: Yoichi Umemoto

"MUJI Loves India"
poster | 1996
p 045
Size: B1
Creative director: Ikko Tanaka, Kazuko Koike
Art director: Masaaki Hiromura
Photographer: Takashi Oyama
Graphic designer: Toshiyuki Kojima
Copywriter: Yoichi Umemoto

"Untouched Color"
poster | 1984
p 038
Size: B1
Creative director: Ikko Tanaka
Photographer: Taishi Hirokawa
Graphic designer: Masaaki Hiromura
Copywriter: Kazuko Koike

"MUJI: Also Found in Portugal"
poster | 1994
p 042
Size: B1
Creative director: Ikko Tanaka, Kazuko Koike
Art director: Masaaki Hiromura
Photographer: Takashi Oyama
Graphic designer: Toshiyuki Kojima
Copywriter: Yoichi Umemoto

"Essential Quality"
poster | 1997
p 046
Size: B1
Creative director: Ikko Tanaka, Kazuko Koike
Art director: Masaaki Hiromura
Photographer: Noritoyo Nakamoto
Graphic designer: Toshiyuki Kojima
Copywriter: Yoichi Umemoto

"Until Now, and From Now On"
poster | 1984
p 039
Size: B1
Creative director: Ikko Tanaka
Photographer: Taishi Hirokawa
Graphic designer: Masaaki Hiromura
Copywriter: Kazuko Koike

"What We Learned from India"
poster | 1995
p 043
Size: B1
Creative director: Ikko Tanaka, Kazuko Koike
Art director: Masaaki Hiromura
Photographer: Takashi Oyama
Graphic designer: Toshiyuki Kojima
Copywriter: Yoichi Umemoto

"Essential Features"
poster | 1997
p 047
Size: B1
Creative director: Ikko Tanaka, Kazuko Koike
Art director: Masaaki Hiromura
Photographer: Noritoyo Nakamoto
Graphic designer: Toshiyuki Kojima
Copywriter: Yoichi Umemoto

"A More Loveable Bicycle"
poster | 1993
p 040
Size: B1
Creative director: Ikko Tanaka, Kazuko Koike
Art director: Masaaki Hiromura
Photographer: Kazumi Kurigami
Graphic designer: Toshiyuki Kojima
Copywriter: Yoichi Umemoto

"Made from a Woman's Point of View"
poster | 1996
p 044
Size: B1
Creative director: Ikko Tanaka, Kazuko Koike
Art director: Masaaki Hiromura
Photographer: Taishi Hirokawa
Graphic designer: Toshiyuki Kojima
Copywriter: Yoichi Umemoto

"The MUJI Wind Blows in London and Paris"
poster | 2000
p 049
Size: B1
Art director: Ikko Tanaka
Graphic designer: Hiroshi Yamamoto
Copywriter: Kazuko Koike
Illustrator: Yuzo Yamashita

MUJI Glasgow
1992 (closed 1995)
pp 050-051

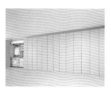

MUJI HOUSE (Renovation)
2004 | pp 056-057
Product designer: Tokujin Yoshioka
Photo:
Art director: Kenya Hara
Photographer: Asuka Katagiri
*For all pages onward until p 081

Power Strip
2006
Extension cord, Short-type
2008
p 058

left to right
Maracas, Mini-Xylophone, Guiro, Bell, Castanet
2007
p 062

Organic Cotton Pile Bear-Bracelet
Organic Cotton Pile Bear-Mascot
2007
p 062

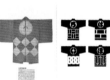

MUJIRUSHI no Hon (Book of MUJI)
Published by Libro Port, Tokyo
1988
pp 052-055
Art director: Ikko Tanaka
Editor in chief: Kazuko Koike
Photographer:
Noritoyo Nakamoto, p 052, p 053 middle,
p 054 top, p 055 top left and middle
Masao Ota, p 053 above left
Takashi Sekiguchi, p 053 top right
Mitsumasa Fujitsuka, p 054 middle
Takashi Hatakeyama, p 054 below left,
p 055 top right
Taishi Hirokawa, p 054 bottom right
Tejbir Singh, p 055 bottom
Graphic designer:
Seigo Kaneko, Taro Matsuyoshi
Editors:
Kazui Kawakami, Hisako Yunoki,
Momoko Takeuchi
Supervisor: Shoji Usami
Producers:
Susumu Takeda, Akimichi Mishima,
Masao Kiuchi, Hideyuki Kuroda, Kiyoshi Okada,
Hikaru Onuma, Hiroshi Nogami, Toshio Goto

Cherry Finish Hall Coat Tree Stand, L
Cherry Finish Hall Coat Tree Stand, S
2006
p 059

PP Airtight Container / 6L
PP Airtight Container / 20L
PP Airtight Container / 45L
2006
p 059

Linen Caftan
2006
pp 060-061

House Type Gift Box / L
House Type Gift Box / M
2008
p 062

Long-Sleeved Pajamas with a Belly Band / sax
blue
2007
p 063

Ash Bed—Double Bed
Headboard for Ash Bed
2008
p 064

26-inch Bicycle
2009
p 065

Skin Toning Lotion for Sensitive Skin
High-Moisturizing Action
2008
p 067

Beige Porcelain Ladle Stand
2007
Stainless Steel Ladle
2005
p 071

Electrical Fan
2008
p 065

Polyethylene Hot Water Bottle / L
Polyethylene Hot Water Bottle / S
2008
p 067

Steam Fan-Type Aroma Humidifier
2008
p 071

Stainless Steel Non-Chlorofluocarbon
Refrigerator / 375L
2007
p 066
Product designer: Naoto Fukasawa

Stainless Steel 5-Shelf Wide Unit
Stainless Steel 5-Shelf Narrow Unit
Stainless Steel 4-Shelf Wide Unit
Stainless Steel 5-Shelf Narrow Unit
Stainless Steel 3-Shelf Wide Unit
Stainless Steel 3-Shelf narrow unit
2005, pp 068-069

Rattan Stackable Basket / Small
Rattan Stackable Box / Small
Rattan Stackable Basket / Large
2007
p 072

Recycled Double Cotton Key Neck Shirt / Gray
2008
p 067

PP System Box: Lids for Dust Bin/
Recycling Separator/Umbrella Stand
2006
p 070

Canvas Tote Bag
2010
p 072
Product designer: Naoto Fukasawa

Steel Frame
2008
PP Single Drawer DVD Unit
2006
Steel Frame Type
2008
p 067

Aluminum Doorknob with Key
Aluminum Lever Handle with Key
2007
p 070

4-Drawer Steel Unit with Castors
9-Drawer Steel Unit with Castors
2006
p 072

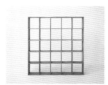

Stacking Oak Shelf, 5-Shelf
Stacking Oak Shelf, 5-Shelf (Additional shelf set)
2009
p 073
Photographer: Asuka Katagiri
*For all pages onward until p 081

Recycled Kraft Paper Memo Pad
1996
p 077

Wall-Mounted CD Player / White
2004
p 083
Product designer: Naoto Fukasawa
Photographer: Tamotsu Fujii

Relaxation Chair with An Ottoman, Upholstered with An Acrylic Blend Plain-Weave Sofa Cover
2009
pp 074-075
Product designer: Naoto Fukasawa

Organic Unbleached Cotton Pile Towels
2008
p 077

Rice Cooker 0.5L
2005
Bamboo Rice Paddle
2002
p 085
Product designer: Naoto Fukasawa
Photographer: Hidetoyo Sasaki, inter office ltd. (hhstyle.com)
*For all pages onward until p 086

Jute Bag
2008
p 076

Mattress-Bed
1991
pp 078-079

Air Cleaner
2007
p 086
Product designer: Naoto Fukasawa

Unsalted Potato Chips Wave-Cut Type
2009
p 077

Wooden Hexagonal Mechanical Pencil
Wooden Hexagonal Ball Point
2009
Aluminum Ball Point Pen
Aluminum Mechanical Pencil
2000
Pencil
2007
pp 080-081

Shredder
2007
PP Dust Box for Shredder
2004
PP Dust Box
2001
p 087
Product designer: Naoto Fukasawa
Photographer: Nacása & Partners Inc.

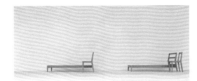

Ash Bed—Double Bed
Ash Chair
2004
pp 088-089
Product designer: Naoto Fukasawa
Photographer: Yoshihiko Ueda
*For all pages onward until p 109

Solid Oak Dining Table
2007 | pp 095-099
Product designer: Naoto Fukasawa

Fabric Upholstery Sofa with Oak Legs
Fabric Upholstery Sofa Cover in Hemp Canvas
2007
p 103
Product designer: Jasper Morrison
Photographer: Yoshihiko Ueda
*For all pages onward until p 109

Molded Sofa with Left Arm
Molded Sofa with Right Arm
Cotton Upholstery Sofa Cover for Molded Sofa
Cotton Upholstery Sofa Cover for Molded Sofa
2005
p 090-091
Product designer: Jasper Morrison

Solid Oak Side Cabinet
2008
p 100
Product designer: Naoto Fukasawa

Steel Shelf
2007
pp 104-105
Product designer: Konstantin Grcic

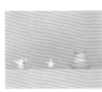

left to right
Bone China Milk Creamer
Bone China Tea Pot / L
Bone China 14cm Plate and Saucer
2006
Bone China Coffee Cup
2005
Hakuji Porcelain Tea Pot
Hakuji Porcelain Soy Sauce Pot
Hakuji Porcelain Rice Bowl / L
Hakuji Porcelain Round Flat Bowl / L
Hakuji Porcelain *Donburi* Bowl/L
Hakuji Porcelain Bowl
Hakuji Porcelain Plate / L
Hakuji Porcelain Plate / XL
2004
pp 092-093
Product designer: Masahiro Mori

Center: Solid Oak Bench, Stock
Left and Right: Custom-Made Solid Oak Benches
2007
p 101
Product designer: Naoto Fukasawa

Tube Chair with A Back Cushion
2007
p 105
Product designer: Konstantin Grcic

Wide-Arm 3-Seater Sofa—Double Feather Cushion
Cotton Upholstery Wide-Arm Sofa Cover
for Double Feather Cushion / Off white
2007
p 102

Oak Oval Dining Table
2007 | pp 106-109
Product designer: Jasper Morrison

Beech Bentwood Chair With Wooden Seat / Brown
p 111, p 112, p 113
Beech Table / Brown / Large
2009
p 112
Product designer: James Irvine
Photographer: Takashi Sekiguchi
*For all pages onward until p 117

MUJI Milano Salone
concept book | 2003
pp 122-127
Size: W265 x H210mm, 32pages
Art director: Kenya Hara
Photographer: Tamotsu Fujii
Graphic designer: Kenya Hara, Izumi Suge

"MUJI and the Teahouse" Campaign
newspaper ad | 2005
pp 132-133
Size: W787 x H511
Art director: Kenya Hara
Photographer: Yoshihiko Ueda
Copywriter: Kenya Hara
Graphic designer: Kenya Hara, Izumi Suge
Cooperator: Sooku Sen
Coordinator: Mari Hashimoto

Tubular Steel Chair / Dark / Grey
Tubular Steel Desk / Dark Grey / Medium
Tubular Steel Low Table / Dark Grey / Large
Steel Shelf for Tubular Low Table / Dark Grey
2009
pp 114-115, pp 116-117
Product designer: Konstantin Grcic

"Horizon" Campaign, Uyuni Salt Flats, Bolivia
Newspaper ad | 2003
pp 128-129
Size: W787 x H511
Art director: Kenya Hara
Photographer: Tamotsu Fujii
Copywriter: Kenya Hara
Graphic designer: Kenya Hara, Izumi Suge

"MUJI and the Teahouse" Campaign
poster | 2005
pp 134-135
Size: W2912 x H1030mm (B0 x 2)
Art director: Kenya Hara
Photographer: Yoshohiko Ueda
Graphic designer: Kenya Hara, Izumi Suge

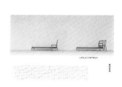

"Horizon" Campaign, Uyuni Salt Flats, Bolivia
pp 118-119
"Horizon" Campaign, Mongolia
pp 120-121
poster | 2003
Size: W2912 x H1030mm (B0 x 2)
Art director: Kenya Hara
Photographer: Tamotsu Fujii
Graphic designer: Kenya Hara, Yukie Inoue,
Izumi Suge
Coodinator: Aoi Advertizing Promotion Inc. /
Kumiko Kitamura, Maho Ikeda

"House" Campaign, Cameroon
"House" Campaign, Morocco
poster | 2004
pp 130-131
Size: W2912 x H1030mm (B0 x 2)
Art director: Kenya Hara
Photographer: Tamotsu Fujii
Graphic designer: Kenya Hara, Yukie Inoue,
Izumi Suge
Coodinator: Aoi Advertizing Promotion Inc. /
Kumiko Kitamura, Kensuke Shiga, Maho Ikeda

"What Happens Naturally" Campaign
newspaper ad | 2006
pp 136-137
Size: W787 x H511
Art director: Kenya Hara
Photographer: Yoshihiko Ueda
Copywriter: Munenori Harada (catch-phrase),
Kenya Hara (body)
Graphic designer: Kenya Hara, Yukie Inoue

"Let's Take Care" Campaign
newspaper ad | 2008
pp 138-139
Size: W787 x H511
Art director: Kenya Hara
Photographer: Yoshihiko Ueda
Copywriter: Munenori Harada (catch-phrase),
Kenya Hara (body)
Graphic designer:
Kenya Hara, Yukie Inoue, Rikako Hayashi

"Like Water" Campaign, Istanbul
"Like Water" Campaign, Beijing
poster | 2009
pp 144-145
Size: W2912 x H1030mm (B0 x 2)
Art director: Kenya Hara
Photographer: Yoshohiko Ueda
Copywriter: Munenori Harada
Graphic designer: Kenya Hara, Yukie Inoue

Revised Tag System, 2008 Version
2008
p 151, p 153
Package:
Art director: Kenya Hara
Graphic designer:
Yukie Inoue, Izumi Suge, Akiko Uematsu

"Let's Take Care" Campaign
poster | 2008
pp 140-141
Size: W2912 x H1030mm (B0 x 2)
Art director: Kenya Hara
Photographer: Yoshohiko Ueda
Copywriter: Munenori Harada
Graphic designer:
Kenya Hara, Yukie Inoue, Rikako Hayashi

Image of "Like Water" Campaign, Rome
2009
pp 146-147
Location: Rome
Art director: Kenya Hara
Photographer: Yoshihiko Ueda

MUJI Catalog
2006
pp 156-157
Size: W148 x H210mm, 32pages
Art director: Kenya Hara
Photographer: Yoichi Nagano
Graphic designer: Kenya Hara, Megumi Nomura
Stylist: Junko Okamoto

"Like Water" Campaign, New York
newspaper ad | 2009
pp 142-143
Size: W787 x H511
Art director: Kenya Hara
Photographer: Yoshihiko Ueda
Copywriter: Munenori Harada (catch-phrase),
Kenya Hara (body)
Graphic designer: Kenya Hara, Yukie Inoue

MUJI Shopping Bag
2010
pp 148-149
Art director: Kenya Hara
Photographer: Takashi Sekiguchi
*For all pages onward until p 153

Magazine Ad
2002
pp 158-159
Size: W230 x H284mm
Art director: Kenya Hara
Photographer: Tamotsu Fujii
Graphic designer:
Kenya Hara, Yukie Inoue, Izumi Suge

List of Sources and Credits

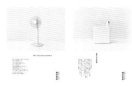

"Making It Beautiful Made It Understated."
Magazine ad | 2008
p 160
"Humidifier with A Chimney."
Magazine ad | 2008
p 161
Size: W230 x H284mm
Art director: Kenya Hara
Photographer: Asuka Katagiri
Graphic designer: Kenya Hara, Megumi Nomura
Copywriter: Meiling Kogure, Chiyoko Namima

MUJI Sapporo Factory
1993
p 175
closed
Interior designer: Takashi Sugimoto

MUJI Shinjuku
2008
pp 190-203
Interior designer: Takashi Sugimoto
Photographer: Akihiro Ito (un, amanagroup)

Exhibition view, Milano Salone
2003
pp 162-169
Creative director:
Takashi Sugimoto, Kenya Hara, Naoto Fukasawa
Collaborative desingner: Tim Power
Photographer:
Tamotsu Fujii (Exhibition Graphic),
Atsushi Nakamichi (Nacása & Partners Inc.)

MUJI Yurakucho
2001
pp 176-183
Interior designer: Takashi Sugimoto, pp 176-177
Photographer:
Akihiro Ito (un, amanagroup), pp 176-177,
pp 178-179
Atsushi Yamahira, pp 180-181, pp 182-183

MUJI to GO, Nagoya Chubu Centrair
International Airport
2009
pp 204-207
Photographer: Megumi Oyama (un, amanagroup)

MUJI Aoyama 3-chome, Tokyo
1993
pp 171-173
Interior designer: Takashi Sugimoto
Photographer: Yoshio Shiratori
*For all pages onward until p 175

MUJI Tokyo Midtown, Roppongi, Tokyo
2007
pp 185-189
Interior designer: Takashi Sugimoto
Photographer:
Yoshio Shiratori, p 185, pp 186-187,
pp 188-189

MUJI Wood House
2005
pp 209-217
Architect: Kazuhiko Namba
Photographer:
Asuka Katagiri, p209, pp 210-211, pp 212-213,
pp 214-215
Mie Morimoto, pp 216-217

MUJI Window House
2007
pp 218-219
Architect: Kengo Kuma
Photographer: Yasuhiro Nakata

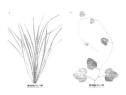

Image from "MUJI Campground" Campaign
poster | 2005
pp 224-225
Size: B1
Art director: Norito Shinmura
Designer: Yuka Watanabe

MUJI BGM (Background Music)
1980 - 2000
pp 230-231
Art director, Designer: Norito Shinmura
Photographer:
Akihiro Miyagi (BGM 2, 3)
Hidetoshi Ochiai (BGM 4)
Naoki Fujioka (BGM 5, 6)

Shiroi Komachi Project
pp 220-221
2010
Architect: Kengo Kuma
Photographer: Shinpei Kato

Image from "MUJI Campground" Campaign
poster | 2008
pp 226-227
Size: B1
Art director: Norito Shinmura
Designer: Kosuke Niwano
Illustrator: Kosuke Niwano

no title
2006
pp 232-233
Art director: Kenya Hara
Photographer: Takashi Sekiguchi

Minami Norikura Campground
Gifu Prefecture
1996
pp 222-223
Tsunan Campground
Niigata Prefecture
1995
p 223
Campagna Tsumagoi Campground
Gunma Prefecture
2004
p 223

Image from "MUJI Campground" Campaign
poster | 2009
pp 228-229
Art director: Norito Shinmura
Designer: Kosuke Niwano
Illustrator: Kosuke Niwano
Size: B1

MUJI furniture in use at the Artist-In-Residence facility of Tokyo Wonder Site, located in Aoyama.
2006
p 239
Art director: Kenya Hara
Photographer: Asuka Katagiri

Contributing Essayists

Jasper MORRISON

———

MUJI is
good for you

Jasper Morrison was born in London in 1959, and graduated in Design at Kingston Polytechnic Design School, London (1979-82 BA (Des.)) and The Royal College of Art for Postgraduate studies (1982-85 MA (Des.) RCA). In 1984 he studied at Berlin's HdK on a Scholarship. In 1986 he set up an Office for Design in London. Today Jasper Morrison Ltd. consists of three design offices, a main office in London and two branch office: one in Paris and one in Tokyo. Services offered by Jasper Morrison Ltd. are wide ranging, from tableware and kitchen products to furniture and lighting, sanitaryware, electronics and appliance design and more recently watches & clocks. Occasionally, Jasper Morrison Ltd. even tackles urban design projects. 2005 saw the founding of Super Normal with Naoto Fukasawa. In June 2006, the first Super Normal exhibition was held in Tokyo. 2009 saw the opening of the Jasper Morrison Limited Shop in London.

John C. JAY

———

MUJI:
Reinventing
the Future

John C. Jay is the Global Executive Creative Director / Partner of the advertising agency, Wieden+Kennedy. Previously, he opened W+K Tokyo and lived in Japan for 6 years where he also launched W+K Tokyo Lab, the independent DVD/CD music label. Prior to W+K, Jay was Creative Director then Marketing Director for fashion retailer, Bloomingdale's in New York City. Jay also oversees Studio J in Portland Oregon, his creative consultancy and studio specializing in product development and design, cultural exhibitions and books, and lifestyle concepts. He was once chosen by I.D. Magazine, as "One of America's 40 most influential designers in the country." His book, *Soul of the Game* received a Gold Medal at the Leipzig Book Fair as well as being named "14 Most beautiful books in the World" by the Copenhagen Museum. He is a partner and co-designer of PING, named by *GQ* as one of "America's Top Ten New Restaurants."

Bruce MAU

———

Meeting MUJI
inspires optimism

Bruce Mau is one of the leading figures in global design. He is the Chief Creative Officer of Bruce Mau Design, with studios in Toronto and Chicago. Mau demonstrates that the power of design is boundless, and has the capacity to bring positive change on a global scale. Inspired by the conviction that the future demands a new breed of designer, Mau founded the Institute without Boundaries. IWB became the engine for *Massive Change*, an ambitious travelling exhibition, publication, and educational series on the power and possibility of design. Bruce Mau is the author of several books, most notably *S,M,L,XL; Lifestyle* and *Massive Change*. His vision of an ethical sustainable future is at the forefront of all of his work.

Authors

Masaaki KANAI

Not "This is what
I want" but
"This will do"

President and Representative Director, MUJI/Ryohin Keikaku Co., Ltd. Born in 1957. Kanai began working for SEIYU Store Nagano, Co., Ltd. (currently Seiyu GK, Co., Ltd.). He transferred to Ryohin Keikaku Co., Ltd. in 1993, and, as the general manager of lifestyle goods, for many years he drove the production of lifestyle goods, the core of sales, and supported the growth of Ryohin Keikaku. Later he became executive director of the sales department and worked with current chairman and representative director Tadamitsu Matsui toward a restructuring of Ryohin Keikaku. In February 2008, Kanai was appointed president and representative director. He has been deeply involved with MUJI since it was a private brand of Seiyu supermarket, working constantly on sales and production. Since August 2006, he has concurrently acted as president of Idée Co., Ltd., a member of the Ryohin Keikaku Group. Kanai continues to work to improve the corporate value of the entire group.

Kazuko KOIKE

The Birth
of MUJI

Photo: Satomi Tomita

Creative Director. Born in Tokyo in 1936. As a founding member of the MUJI advisory board and a copywriter, Koike has played an active part in conceptualizing MUJI. She is the head of MUJI's Laboratory of Superior Items for Living since 2009. From 1983 to 2000, she established and directed Sagacho Exhibit Space, Japan's first alternative space, which has launched the international careers of many Japanese contemporary artists. Koike's curatorial works examine the boundaries between the fields of art, design, and fashion from a standpoint of design research. She has written and edited many books, including *Issey Miyake East Meets West, Japanese Coloring, Japan Design* (art directed by Ikko Tanaka), and *Aura of a Space*. Koike is Professor Emeritus at Musashino Art University.

**Naoto
FUKASAWA**

Product Design
of MUJI

Product Designer. Born in 1956. Fukasawa has been a member of the MUJI advisory board since 2002. He has designed and consulted for representative brands and major companies in Europe and Asia. Based on his own central concept, which he calls, "Without Thought," Fukasawa has been directing workshops to extract designs from unconscious memories and actions. MUJI's wall-mounted CD player, which won the German iF Gold Award and the D&AD Award in 2002 and joined MoMA New York's permanent collection in 2005, was the result of one of these workshops. Fukasawa has received many awards and honors, including the distinction in 2007 of Royal Designer for Industry (from the U.K.'s Royal Society for the Encouragement of Arts, Manufactures and Commerce).

Kenya HARA

Identity and
Communication
of MUJI

Photo: Yoshiaki Tsutsui

Graphic Designer. Born in 1958. Hara has been a member of the MUJI advisory board since 2001. The designs he has developed conceptualize the future of lifestyle and industry. He has planned and produced various international touring exhibitions: RE-DESIGN, HAPTIC, and Japan Car. Hara's exhibition of artificial, high-technology fibers, called SENSEWARE, was displayed at the Milan Triennale 2009 and resulted in a great deal of public interest. Hara also designed the opening/closing ceremony program of the Nagano Olympic Winter Games, as well as the official posters and other promotional collateral for EXPO 2005 Aichi, both of which embody traditional Japanese aesthetics in a contemporary context. Hara's work covers a diverse range of activities and fields and has garnered numerous design awards. Among his works are a fragrance for Kenzo, mobile phone for NTTdocomo, signage system for a hospital, and visual identity for Matsuya department store in Ginza. His books *Designing Design* and *White* have been translated into various languages.

**Takashi
SUGIMOTO**

MUJI Space

Interior designer. Born in Tokyo in 1945. After graduating from Tokyo National University of the Faculty Program of Fine Arts in 1968 Sugimoto established his interior design firm Super Potato in 1973. He is a founding member of the MUJI advisory board, and has acted as designer and supervisor for every MUJI store built since the very first one in Aoyama in 1983. Currently, Sugimoto designs interiors for hotels and restaurants around the world and has extended his field of work to producing environments for commercial complexes. His recent works include: Park Hyatt Seoul and Beijing; Grand Hyatt Singapore, Shanghai, and Tokyo; Hyatt Regency Kyoto and Hakone; Shangri-La Hong Kong, Shanghai, and Bangkok; and Bellagio Las Vegas.

Founding Members of MUJI

Seiji TSUTSUMI

Ikko TANAKA

Kazuko KOIKE

Hiroshi KOJITANI

Takashi SUGIMOTO

Masaru AMANO